River Glory

by

Ruth Ward Heflin

McDougal Publishing is a ministry of The McDougal Foundation, Inc., a Maryland nonprofit corporation
dedicated to spreading the Gospel of the Lord Jesus Christ
to as many people as possible in the shortest time possible.

Published by:

McDougal Publishing
P.O. Box 3595
Hagerstown, MD 21742-3595
www.mcdougal.org

ISBN 1-884369-87-1

Printed in the United States of America
For Worldwide Distribution

Other books by Ruth Ward Heflin:

Glory
Revival Glory
Jerusalem, Zion, Israel and the Nations

About the Title:

One night in the spring of 1998 Sister Jane Lowder spun around on the platform under her prophetic anointing and said to me, "Your next book will be on the river." I knew she was right, and I began preaching on the river every opportunity I got because of that prophetic word.

Dedication

To my mother:

Rev. Edith Ward Heflin

who has known God's glory more fully than anyone else I have known.

THERE IS A RIVER, the streams whereof shall make glad the city of God, the holy place of the tabernacles of the most High. God is in the midst of her; she shall not be moved: God shall help her, and that right early.

Psalm 46:4-5

And when the man that had the line in his hand went forth eastward, he measured a thousand cubits, and he brought me through the waters; the waters were to the ankles. Again he measured a thousand, and brought me through the waters; the waters were to the knees. Again he measured a thousand, and brought me through; the waters were to the loins. Afterward he measured a thousand; and IT WAS A RIVER that I could not pass over: for the waters were risen, waters to swim in, A RIVER That could not be passed over.   Ezekiel 47:3-5

In the last day, that great day of the feast, Jesus stood and cried, saying, If any man thirst, let him come unto me, and drink. He that believeth on me, as the scripture hath said, out of his belly shall flow RIVERS OF LIVING WATER. (But this spake he of the Spirit, which they that believe on him should receive: for the Holy Ghost was not yet given; because that Jesus was not yet glorified.)

John 7:37-39

And he showed me A PURE RIVER of water of life, clear as crystal, proceeding out of the throne of God and of the Lamb.   Revelation 22:1

Contents

Introduction

During the summer of 1998, God gave us as the theme for our summer campmeeting, "Let the River Flow." As the meetings progressed and spiritually hungry people came from all over America and the world, we felt the waters rising, much as Ezekiel had experienced, and God began to give us, through the analogy of the river, a whole new consciousness of His Spirit. It is because God wants us to know the Spirit that He is showing us the river. The theology of the Spirit may be beyond some, but we can all understand the river. The complexities of doctrine may be confusing for some, but we can all learn to flow in the life-giving waters of God's stream.

God wants us to understand the moving of His Spirit and the sometimes very strange way in which He is operating in this last day and hour, and when we can see the moving of the Spirit of God as a great flowing river, we can better understand how to step into it, and how to learn to flow with its currents. If we can understand this great river, we can understand the flow of the Spirit of God, for the river is the Holy Spirit, and the flow of the river is the outpouring of the Holy Spirit that we are experiencing in this day.

In the great river of God we can find everything we need to accomplish His work in these last days. Nothing of what He has called us to is impossible when we submit our will to the will of His great river. This is the time of harvest, and we are about to reap the greatest harvest the world has ever known. We will do it because of the greatness of the river, not because of any greatness of our own.

The fire and the wind and every other aspect of the glory that was revealed to John and Ezekiel and other prophets can be found in the realm of the river. Let us jump in and enjoy all the benefits that await us.

Some are coming to the river because of a pressing personal need, often because they need a healing miracle or a financial miracle. Others are coming because they have a need in their ministry. Never were more demands made on those of us who are involved in ministry, and the burdens placed upon us are often very heavy to bear. Many come simply because of their great thirst for God. Whatever brings us to the river, if we can all get into it, every need will be supplied.

Ruth Ward Heflin
Ashland, Virginia

Part I:

The River

Chapter 1

The River Is Here

Remember ye not the former things, neither consider the things of old. Behold, I will do a new thing; now it shall spring forth; shall ye not know it? I will even make a way in the wilderness, and RIVERS IN THE DESERT. The beast of the field shall honour me, the dragons and the owls: because I GIVE WATERS IN THE WILDERNESS, AND RIVERS IN THE DESERT, to give drink to my people, my chosen. This people have I formed for myself; they shall show forth my praise. Isaiah 43:18-21

"I give waters in the wilderness, and rivers in the desert." Wait no longer; the river is here.

For many years the church has prayed and anxiously awaited another wave of heavenly glory that would lift us out of spiritual lethargy and envelop us with the presence and power of the living God that has been demonstrated in past revivals. Well, the wait is over. God is moving by His Spirit all over the world, and all we have to do is step into the revival. The river is here.

Something wonderful is happening. We are conscious of standing in the waters of a heavenly stream. Some of us have taken only small steps away from the shoreline, but many of us are finding ourselves in deeper and deeper water without having to put forth any effort whatsoever. The river is carrying us out. It's here.

It is no longer difficult for us to move from the ankle-deep water into the knee-deep water and from the knee-deep water into the loin-deep water. It is somehow easy now to move on out into even deeper places, into *"water to swim in."* All we need to do is yield to the river, and the river does the work.

What we are experiencing is so wonderful that sometimes it seems more like a dream than reality. Recently, when I am in special meetings, it seems almost as if my arms don't belong to me. They feel very strange as the Lord possesses them to use for His glory. I sometimes seem to be looking down or looking on as I see what God is doing with my life and for the people. These are wonderful days to be alive. The river is here.

God is doing new things, and I like that. I have

had many wonderful experiences in Him, but unless I am touched in a new way in every service, unless God reveals something to me that I have not known before, unless I have fresh insight, unless I feel the quickening of His Spirit in new ways, I am not satisfied. I am determined to keep reaching into the eternal realm of the Spirit of God, I insist on stepping into new liberty, I refuse to take a single step backward, and I continue to claim new territory in God.

> **God is doing things differently than we could have anticipated. He is sending revival in His own way and is calling for a people who will accept revival on His terms.**

God is doing things differently than we could have anticipated. He is sending revival in His own way and is calling for a people who will accept revival on His terms. Some who have been waiting for revival for years have wanted to have it in their own way. They are now becoming so hungry, however, that they are willing to have it on God's terms. Hunger makes you willing to yield to God's flow.

People are coming to our campmeetings from all

over the world and sitting in our open-air tabernacle because they are so hungry for God. Many of those who have attended conferences in recent years have never been in a major conference which had no air-conditioning. Our campground is a missionary training center, and when we go out to Africa and India and the Isles of the Sea, we don't find air-conditioning in many places, so we need this training. Still, in spite of the rather basic conditions of the camp, people are willing to come because they are so hungry, and they have heard that the river is with us.

When we began to have our women's conferences and our men's conferences, people would call and ask who the speakers would be and base their decision about coming on the answer. Now, they no longer do that. God's river goes beyond personalities. When the river of God's Spirit is flowing, it doesn't matter who the speaker is. God does the work. Now people come because they want to be in the atmosphere of the glory. If the glory of God is present, nothing else matters. The river is here.

We have not been able to predict exactly how God would bring revival to any specific area. We have found it best just to stand back and watch it all happen, to let the flood of God's glory pour forth into our desert places. Revival is in the river, and the river is here.

The same Spirit that moved upon the face of the waters in the book of Genesis and the same Spirit that descended upon the one hundred and twenty believers on the Day of Pentecost in Jerusalem is ready to bring forth revival in your town and in your church and in your household if you will just let Him do it. The result will be beyond anything you have ever experienced, so don't be surprised and don't be scandalized. Let it flow.

As young Pentecostal ministers, we were taught that before we went out to minister to someone seriously ill, we had to spend time in prayer and get ourselves spiritually built up. While living as a missionary in Hong Kong, one day I was called upon to pray for a lady dying of cancer, and I didn't have time to spend with God in prayer before I went. On my way to the hospital, I said to the Lord, "Lord, You know I haven't had time to pray about this. This is an emergency situation."

The Lord answered me, "I didn't call you to be a reservoir. I called you to be an open channel so that My life could flow out through you."

When I got to the hospital, I felt nothing unusual in my hands. I said, "Lord I am extending my hand as an act of faith that You will heal this woman." By the time my hand got to the sick woman's head, the power of God was surging through it, and that hand was shaking so much that I was nearly embarrassed by it. God was letting me know that the river was present and that it would do its work.

The woman was instantly healed. She had not been able to get out of bed for many weeks, but now she got up and walked with me all the way down the corridor to where I had to get the elevator to go back down.

You don't have to feel "full of glory" all the time. You can be an empty riverbed. Just let the river of God flow through you.

Don't wait on others. Let the rhythms of the river begin to come into your spirit. Let God give you a greater sensitivity to His Spirit, and, as the river begins to flow, allow yourself to be carried away by it. Stop clinging to the shoreline. I know we are afraid of the unknown, but there is no reason to fear God. Let Him carry you away from the realm of your natural thinking. Let Him carry you away into the depths of the river.

These waters will carry you to the place of miracles and signs and wonders.

As the waters begin to rise, don't get panicky. These waters will carry you to the place of miracles and signs and wonders. Relax in the waters. Let them bring you into a miraculous realm beyond anything you have witnessed in the past.

Some people who come to us for prayer for their bodies want to tell us exactly how to pray for them. At times I have to say, "Excuse me. Don't talk anymore. You are breaking the flow of the river." God doesn't need us to tell Him how to do everything. He is perfectly capable. Just relax and go with the flow of the river, for the river is here.

Can we have the power of God just as they did on the Day of Pentecost? Of course we can — if we will just get out of God's way and let the river flow. Can we have the power of God just as men and women did at Azusa Street in the early 1900s? Of course we can. Can we have the power of God that was demonstrated in the 1948 revival or in the great Charismatic Renewal? Of course we can. God hasn't changed. Let the river flow.

When Pentecostals stopped letting the river flow, the miracles stopped too. Break up the dams that hinder the flow of the river and the miracles will return to the Church. We are the ones who have changed, not God. Let Him have His way, and He will do signs and wonders in our midst.

God refuses to be our servant, to heed our every capricious whim. He is God. Why should He do it any other way? Let the river flow. Stop telling God what to do and when to do it and let Him do it His own way — by the Spirit. It is time to step into the depths of the river and to go with its flow.

There are many things that God wants to do for us in the depths of the river which we will not be able to analyze. We must just accept them. The waters of God's river are refreshing, cleansing and empowering. That should be enough. Just don't stop with the refreshing stage and don't be satisfied with the cleansing stage. Move on into the empowerment of the river. It's here.

> There are many things that God wants to do for us in the depths of the river which we will not be able to analyze. We must just accept them.

God is calling each of us to know and live in the heavenly realm, and we can. This was the realm Jesus lived in while He was on the Earth. He only did what He saw the Father doing:

> *Then answered Jesus and said unto them, Verily, verily, I say unto you, The Son can do nothing of himself, but what he seeth the Father do: for what things soever he doeth, these also doeth the Son likewise.*   John 5:19

Jesus only said what the Father said. He was connected to the heavenly realm. That is why He taught us to pray the prayer, *"Thy will be done on Earth as it is in Heaven."* Get into the heavenly realm, this realm of the glory of God, and be carried away so that you can see the Father and hear the Father in the realm of the Spirit. What you see Him doing and hear Him saying will be a guide for your actions and words. Jump in. The river is here.

As our summer progressed in 1998, the flow of the river was so great that some people went home to get others and bring them back. Buses were chartered, and busloads of spiritually hungry people were brought to the camp. It was like that all summer long.

God had warned me to prepare for it. When we started to pave a new section of the parking lot, those who were doing it asked me if I would like to use a better grade of asphalt. "It is more expensive," they told me, "but it can support buses."

"You're prophesying," I said. God knew that we would need it.

I was concerned that we didn't have enough room in the open-air tabernacle for everyone to stretch out in the Spirit at one time. I didn't want anyone to get hurt by one person falling on top of another. The Lord showed me to put a cement walkway on both sides of the platform at the same level and to carpet it. We could then go up and down that walkway praying for people. In every way we could, we were getting ready for revival.

Two weeks before campmeeting started the Lord woke me up one morning and told me to call the bank and borrow money for two new vans. We had always bought cheap vans at auction that had a little life left in them. The Lord was showing us that with the increase in activity we now needed something better. "If you don't do it today," the Lord told me, "the vans won't be here in time."

I hadn't even looked at vans, but I called the bank to ask if they would loan us the money for two. The loan officer told me it shouldn't be a problem and that I should go ahead and look around for what we wanted.

We called around to the dealers and found that there were only two vans of that type available in the city. We asked the dealers to send them out for us to see. The second van did not arrive until about four-thirty in the afternoon. Since there were only two vans available and God had told us to buy two vans, I was sure that these must be the two vans God wanted us to buy. I got to the bank about five o'clock, and the papers were drawn up and ready to sign by five-thirty. After that day, time was very limited for us, even in half-hour segments. I would not have had time if I had not obeyed the Lord when He spoke to me.

Strange new things are happening all around us. Get your foot on the starting line and be ready to launch forth at a moment's notice. The river is here.

Some believers are seriously thinking about leaving the churches they have been attending because they are tired of waiting for revival to come. This, however, is not the time to leave. The river is rising. Some people have been contemplating leaving ministries with which they have been involved for some time because they have not seen their prayers answered nor their gifts developed there. But don't leave now. The waters are rising. That church will need you in the near future. The leaders of that ministry will need your help when they find themselves swimming in deeper waters. We are all about to be amazed by the scope of what God will do in the very near future. The river is here.

Some believers are seriously thinking about leaving the churches they have been attending because they are tired of waiting for revival to come. This, however, is not the time to leave. The river is rising.

My friend, Debbie Kendrick, had a wonderful vision in February of 1998. She saw a group of buildings. One building was an unfinished house that she understood represented a certain ministry. It was built over a strong, well-planned foundation, but it had never been finished. Although it lacked a roof, the minister in charge of it had decided to live on the second floor.

The next building she saw was a strong and tall tower. She described it as being "very much like the tower at the Plaza of San Marco in Venice, Italy." It was built so straight and tall that those of us who climbed it could see far over the horizon and know when the river was coming. She saw several of us at the top of it, tiny because of its height, and we were excitedly calling out, "The river is coming! The river is coming!"

There were other buildings built on stilts. Later it became apparent why. All the buildings were built on sand, soil suitable for a river bed, but most wanted to avoid the flood that would surely come. They were doing all they could to keep themselves from getting wet.

As the waters came, she saw that some who had just come into the things of God and who had not yet been able to build their ministries were at an advantage. They were right on the river bed, ready to be carried away in the river.

The man who had made himself a dwelling place on the second floor of his unfinished building was so preoccupied with finishing the building that he didn't even see the river coming and never got wet at all. She heard God tell him to abandon the house and come down. If he didn't, the water would pass him by completely.

Those of us who were on top of the tower and had seen the river coming descended rapidly and got into its waters. Everyone had to come down to get in the river, everyone got in at the same place, and everyone got in together. The river is here. Come down and get into it.

When Benny Hinn was preaching in Detroit in 1998, he had a vision in which he saw a great tidal wave of glory coming in. Although he saw that the hand of the Lord held back two-thirds of the tidal wave and only sent a third of it, he has experienced greater miracles and signs and wonders since then in his meetings.

The river is here, and it is time for you to discover *River Glory*.

Chapter 2

The Vastness of the River

*Afterward he measured a thousand; and it was
A RIVER THAT I COULD NOT PASS
OVER: for the waters were risen, waters to
swim in, A RIVER THAT COULD NOT BE
PASSED OVER.*   Ezekiel 47:5

"A river that could not be passed over..." There is a
vastness to this river that most of us have yet to discover.

The prophet started out in waters up to his ankles,
but it wasn't long before those waters began to rise.
Soon he was up to his knees, then he was up to his
loins, and before he knew it, he had to start swimming because he suddenly found himself in a vast
river. This was not just any river. It was *"a river that
could not be passed over."*

There are great rivers in the world, and they are

long and wide. This river, however, was different. It was unique. It was not like any other the prophet had ever seen. This was the unfathomable river of God.

Good swimmers delight in challenging mighty rivers. They practice for long periods of time, learn to pace themselves and always keep someone nearby in a boat to help them in case they get into trouble. They regularly attempt to swim across the great rivers, and they often succeed. As wide and as deep as those rivers might be, they can be conquered.

When you start wading out into God's waters, however, you soon discover something. There is no other shore in sight. This river is endless. It *cannot be passed over.* Every other river has a right bank and a left bank, but not the river of God. There is no other bank. This river has a beginning, but it has no ending. It has no limits. It never runs its course. Its vastness cannot be measured.

Many of us have a certain smugness about our experience in God. We have been to enough seminars and conferences that we consider ourselves to be authorities on many spiritual subjects. We are authorities on the Holy Spirit, on life in the Spirit, on the gifts of the Spirit, on the healing ministry, on the authority of the believer. "Been there! Done that!" is a commonly-heard remark that expresses the smugness that many feel. We have checked off, point by point, the things we wanted to learn, and our progress is so substantial we somehow feel like we have "made it."

> When you get in touch with the river of God, the first thing you notice is how vast it is. It only takes a few measurements from Heaven to quickly get you out over your head, and you suddenly find yourself swimming. It doesn't take long at all to realize that this river has no boundaries, no limits, and we are only beginning to explore the vastness of it.

This just shows how little we know. When you get in touch with the river of God, the first thing you notice is how vast it is. It only takes a few measurements from Heaven to quickly get you out over your head, and you suddenly find yourself swimming. It doesn't take long at all to realize that this river has no boundaries, no limits, and we are only beginning to explore the vastness of it.

An attitude of smugness in regard to spiritual

matters suggests that a person has, in reality, only begun to know God's river. They are still in the initial stages. They have gotten into the water only up to their ankles or up to their knees or maybe up to their loins. If they had gotten any deeper, they would surely have realized by now that they were just beginning to experience the vastness of God's waters. Although it is only a small step in the Spirit from *"waters ... to the loins"* to *"a river that cannot be passed over,"* we have only touched the surface so far, and we have a very long way to go. This river is vast.

There is a broadness to this river that none of us has yet perceived, and we can only perceive it as we allow God to take us out into it. Cooperate with Him.

When my older sister Betty was still a little girl, she was visiting with our Uncle Bill and Grandma Ward in the Rhode Island area. She had never seen the ocean, so Uncle Bill took her to the shores of the Atlantic and let her splash around in it for a while. When she got back to his house, she ran to her grandmother and said, "Grandma, I have been clear across the ocean today." In her childlike simplicity, her experience that day seemed vast. Some of us are just like that. We think we have been clear across the river of God when the truth is that we haven't gotten very far from the shoreline yet.

There is a broadness to this river that none of us has yet perceived, and we can only perceive it as we allow God to take us out into it. Cooperate with Him. The waters of His river are rising. Let the river carry you away into its depths.

As I said, some find the vastness of this river to be terrifying, but why would we ever fear God's Spirit? He always leads us in great gentleness. Nothing that God has for us need cause us to be afraid. We should see God's river as an exciting challenge. The vastness of it assures us of continual new experiences in His Spirit. We have been wrong to limit God to certain experiences.

Because this river is limitless, we cannot ignore it. We must come to terms with it, and we cannot avoid it, so don't even try. God will not permit you to skip around this river. The waters are rising, and you must decide what you will do with them.

No pastor in America can afford to ignore this river. It is impossible to simply let things continue as they have been in our churches. The river is flowing. Jump in and discover the vastness of *River Glory*.

Chapter 3

The Source of the River

And he showed me a pure river of water of life,
clear as crystal, PROCEEDING OUT OF THE
THRONE OF GOD AND OF THE LAMB.
                                                    Revelation 22:1

"Proceeding out of the throne of God and of the
Lamb ..." John was able to identify the Source of
God's river.

This is a *"pure"* river; it is a *"river ... of life,"* it is
"clear as crystal," and it is coming *"out of the throne of*
God." We know what the river is like, and we know
the Source of it.

We have always found rivers to be intriguing. In
pioneer times, men and women were obsessed with
finding the source of each river, and those who
risked their lives to survey and map the source of
the great rivers became heroes to all succeeding
generations.

Rivers are no less important to us in the time in which we are living. Water — clean water, drinkable water, as well as water for the irrigation of agricultural lands and for use in manufacturing — is one of the major problems the world is now facing. The nation of Israel has struggled with the issue of water rights from its inception. The country has very limited water supplies and is presently looking into the possibility of bringing water from Turkey or Lebanon or even Syria. Many other countries have similar problems, either because of their climate, the growth of their population or the pollution of existing streams. The major treaties of the future will not only concern themselves with war and peace, but with this urgent question of water rights. What will be the source of the water needed by future generations?

The river of God has a unique source. It comes forth directly from His throne. One day in our camp-meeting in the summer of 1998, someone had a vision of the river coming out of the innermost part of the Lord and flowing directly to us. He is the Source of the river, because He is the river.

Because of its unique Source, this river is different from any other. Some rivers are fresh and plentiful at their source, but the farther you get downstream from the source, the more polluted and depleted the waters become. When you are in the river of God, however, you are always at the Source. It comes forth from Him.

Any time you get into God's river, you are standing at the Source. That is why we are called to focus our attention on the river.

With other rivers, although there is a source, a starting point, other water empties into the river at various points downstream, until the resulting mixture of water is not the same as it was at the source. It is not as pure and not as clear. The waters of the Jordan River, for instance, originate in Dan. When the river reaches the areas where pilgrims commonly enter it to be baptized, the water is quite different from the water coming from Dan. God's river is not like this. No matter where you are in this river, its water is fresh and *"pure"* and directly from the Source. There is no contamination, no mixing of other waters. Any time you get into God's river, you are standing at the Source. That is why we are called to focus our attention on the river. Its source is God.

It often happens that certain aspects of revival become tainted by the interpretation men place on them. We always want to understand revival from the point of view of our particular doctrinal position. After a certain aspect of revival has been interpreted and taught enough times, we can barely recognize it. It seems somehow changed. When you consider what is being taught, you have to consider the source of it. That may make all the difference in the world.

This river of God can never be changed. It is pure because its Source is pure. No man can contaminate it with interpretation or bias. No man can twist it to his own liking, to fit his own patterns.

This river of God can never be changed. It is pure because its Source is pure. No man can contaminate it with interpretation or bias. No man can twist it to his own liking, to fit his own patterns. This river *"proceeds out of the throne of God."*

God's river is always full of life. The Jordan runs into the Dead Sea, and because the Dead Sea has no outlet, the water dies. There is no life in the Dead Sea, and that's why it is named as it is.

God's river is always flowing. Nothing can stop

it up. Nothing can prevent it from sending forth more fresh water. Nothing can hinder its flow. Therefore the waters of the river of God are always life-giving.

Some people seem to be stagnated. They are consumed with pointing out the errors of anyone involved with revival, but until they get an anointing as great as revivalists have experienced — until they have a single service in which three hundred stretcher cases are healed, until they have a service in which every crippled person gets out of a wheel chair and walks — they have no right to criticize God's revival.

Why is it necessary to speak of a mistake some great servant of God made years after being used of God in revival? Some people would have talked about Moses in his old age, so God just took him. Rather than let a new generation dissect his dead body, God sent angels to carry it away. It is possible to contaminate revival by our careless words.

I love to speak of past revivals, but what interests me are the miracles God performed, the signs and wonders He showed and the glory that was manifested in the midst of the people. That excites and encourages me to believe for greater miracles. Hearing about mistakes people made doesn't help anyone. Get into the life-giving flow of the river and your waters will not become stagnant.

It is wonderful to watch people who have never before prophesied. Sometimes they don't even know the Scriptures well, yet they sound as if they were Jeremiah or Isaiah. It happens because the Source of the river is also the Giver of the word. It was He who inspired and brought forth the written Word, and because He is in us and we are in Him, what He did for the prophets of old can happen to us as well. It happens when the river is flowing and when we get in position to receive from the Source.

Since the Source of the river is God, and since this river emanates from His throne, it is time for us to get to know both Him and His throne better.

If we want to be pure, we must get into this pure river, and if we want to remain pure, we must stay close to the Source.

The river God showed John is still a *"pure"* river, it is still *"clear as crystal,"* and it is still *"proceeding from the throne of God."* This river is the same in Ashland, Virginia, in Smithton, Missouri, in Brownsville, Florida, or in Toronto, Canada. It is the same in your town, and when you step into it you can expect the same purity and the same crystal clarity still *"proceeding from the throne"* to flow over you, bringing *River Glory* to your life.

Chapter 4

The Power of the River

And it shall come to pass, that EVERY THING THAT LIVETH, WHICH MOVETH, WHITHERSOEVER THE RIVERS SHALL COME, SHALL LIVE ... AND EVERY THING SHALL LIVE WHITHER THE RIVER COMETH.   Ezekiel 47:9

"And every thing shall live whither the river cometh." There is great power in these waters.

The river of God offers much more than we sometimes realize. It gives more than divine healing; it offers divine health, divine life. This river is powerful. Everything in its path is changed.

Divine healing is wonderful, but it is even better to have divine health, divine life flowing through you. I have been very blessed in this regard. The river can keep us so healthy that we hardly know what sickness is. In our ministry team, we all experience a very occasional cold or headache, but never any serious sickness. There is no way to explain this other than to say that the river of God is powerful. It has divine life in it, and when we flow in that life, it touches us physically as well.

Healing has been part of every revival, but we are about to see a healing revival beyond anything seen until this time. In this move of the Spirit, we will experience one hundred percent success in praying for those who are sick: *"Every thing shall live whither the river cometh."*

In many parts of America, the church has gotten away from ministering physical healing. This seems very unusual to me. My parents had great compassion and faith for the sick. When they first came to Richmond to start a church, every new member of that church came in because of a miracle of healing, and many of those healings were very unusual and drew a lot of attention.

After the Richmond congregation was well established, at least ten years passed in which not one member of my parents' church died. Some did get sick, and sometimes their sicknesses were serious, but Daddy and Mother were always called to pray for them, and after they had prayed, the people always recovered.

In Pentecost in general, healing was an expected manifestation here in our American churches until

Medicare came into being. After Medicare was enacted, elderly believers, who would previously have called for the elders of the church to pray over them (with the expected result that they would be healed), suddenly began to call the Rescue Squad instead. Since that time, unless people are dying, they rarely bother the preacher with their sicknesses. They count on Medicare and health insurance to take care of their medical needs.

> There is life and power in the river, and if we apply the healing power of its waters we would have a greater quality of life. Learn to come to the Lord's river first.

Sometimes we are forced to believe God, and I am sure that this will happen more and more in the future. We need, however, to think of the Lord *before* we get on our deathbeds. There is life and power in the river, and if we apply the healing power of its waters we would have a greater quality of life. Learn to come to the Lord's river first.

Sometimes, when we find our brooks suddenly dried up, we will know that God has a purpose in allowing it. Elijah was dependent upon the brook

Cherith, but when that resource was not available, he found that God had another plan. If Medicare should fail us, we will know that God delights in healing His people.

Sometimes people are in and out of the hospital before their pastor even knows they are sick. This should not be. God wants to send another wave of healing glory to the Church today. There is power in the river of God.

> The greatest miracles take place in an atmosphere of great worship and great liberty. If we desire to see great miracles, we must gather together in simplicity, praise the Lord until the spirit of worship comes and worship Him until the glory comes.

The greatest miracles take place in an atmosphere of great worship and great liberty. If we desire to see great miracles, we must gather together in simplicity, praise the Lord until the spirit of worship comes and worship Him until the glory comes. It is then, in that glory, that we will begin to see healings, miracles, and signs and wonders taking place.

A great healing flow is coming, and wherever the

river goes, we will see divine life being imparted. This river brings healing to the emotions, healing to the body and deliverance to the soul. It often happens so quickly and so powerfully that we have difficulty perceiving it.

We have been hearing a lot lately about water therapy, and this is the ultimate water therapy. Karen Sandvick, an award-winning photographer from Mt. Dora, Florida, attended our campmeeting four years ago. As she danced in the Spirit every night and flowed in the river, she was conscious that God was freeing her from her past. She went directly from Virginia to Jerusalem and began serving the Lord. Later, God took her to some of the former Soviet nations to help bring Jewish people home to Israel. She is greatly used of God, and it all started in that flow of the river. What wonderful therapy!

There is healing in these waters. *"Everything that liveth, which moveth, whithersoever the river shall come shall live."* Whatever is touched by the river will live. Every part of your being will come alive in God, and there will be no death in you. No part of your being will be "unwell." Through the work of the river, you will be experiencing a glorious healing flow.

We are about to see very unusual miracles. We have experienced many creative miracles in our meetings in India and Africa where people have very simple faith, but we are beginning to see this type of miracle in America as well. Several people I have prayed for recently who had serious medical conditions went back to their doctors for a checkup and found that they were healed. Some have had the restoration of organs that were removed many years before. X rays supported the testimony of their miracle. We will see many more miracles of this type in the days ahead.

Whatever is touched by the river will live. Every part of your being will come alive in God, and there will be no death in you. No part of your being will be unwell. Through the work of the river, you will be experiencing a glorious healing flow.

Often, God gives us a foretaste of what is to come and, in a moment of glory, shows us what to expect later. This taste stirs a hunger in our hearts and spirits and makes us know that we can go after what we have seen in a new way. I have been declaring this now for many years.

I am not afraid to declare further that we will soon experience a healing revival that will surpass what happened in the great healing revivals of the past century. It will surpass the meetings of Aimee Semple McPherson, of Dr. Charles Price, of Katherine Kuhlman, of A.A. Allen, of Jack Coe and of other great ministers of God. It will happen because we are living in the last days and the glory of the Church will not be less than it has been in days gone by. It will be greater.

As we move on into the twenty-first century, we will see things far greater than we have experienced in this past century. This Church age will not end with a whimper. Revival fires are stirring, and we are seeing unusual signs and wonders wrought by the mighty hand of God. This is only the beginning. Pat Robertson recently had crowds of nearly half a million people in Hyderabad in India with supernatural manifestations of God, and there is an ever-increasing glory evident in Benny Hinn's meetings.

The estimated crowd in attendance at his meeting on the steps of the Capital Building during the Washington for Jesus rally was two hundred and fifty thousand and great things were accomplished for the Kingdom of God. His recent meeting in Bogota, Colombia drew crowds of eighty thousand and more and great miracles were recorded. These same types of miracles will happen for many lesser-known servants of God as well in the days ahead.

The Lord spoke to us last year that the big trees of

the forest must not overshadow the little trees and prevent them from growing. The older, more mature ministries must make way for younger ministries to develop and flourish.

My uncle, Mother's brother, Dr. William A. Ward, published a new book in 1998 called *Miracles That I Have Seen.* I had heard him tell many of the stories he recorded in his book, but some of them were even new to me. When the book first came out, I was very busy getting ready to go overseas, but I couldn't resist opening it at random and reading a few pages. The story I opened to first was about a meeting he conducted in the Bahamas. The first night of his meeting there were three or four blind people present, and they were all healed. The people were so excited that the next day they went in search of blind people to invite. That night they brought more than two hundred blind people to the meeting. He prayed for every one of them, and all except four or five were healed.

The congregation was so excited by these miracles that they looked for greater challenges for the Lord. They asked Uncle Bill to go with them to a local leper colony. When they got there, a medical officer tried to refuse them entry. "I'm very sorry," he said, "but this is a contagious disease. You can't go in and lay your hands on these people because you might contract leprosy. If you like, I will bring out a few, but

even then, you will have to stand back from them."
He marked a line fifty feet away and asked the ministers to stand behind that line as they prayed. In this way, Uncle Bill prayed for fifty-six lepers.

As he was finishing his prayer, he felt led to remember those who had not been allowed out, those who were too sick to be even that close to others. "Heal them as well," he prayed.

Many felt the touch of God, but the medical officer had a very strict policy on releasing his patients. No leper could be declared cured until he had been examined once every two weeks for a whole year. If, after that time, there seemed to be no more symptoms of leprosy, that person could be released.

A little more than a year later, Uncle Bill was attending a meeting where Brother David Nunn was preaching and heard the preacher tell about an evangelist who had gone to the Bahamas, prayed for a group of lepers, and one hundred lepers were healed. Uncle Bill went to Brother Nunn and said, "I am sure I was the evangelist you were talking about, but I only remember praying for fifty-six lepers." Later he called to speak with the pastor who had taken him to that leper colony. He told him what he had heard in David Nunn's meeting and asked him what had actually happened. "I only remember praying for fifty-six people," he repeated.

"Brother Ward," the pastor replied, "do you remember that when you finished praying for the fifty-six lepers outside you also prayed for those who could not come out? Altogether, a hundred lepers were healed, and they closed the leprosarium." Oh, praise God, we will see it again and again in the days just ahead.

My brother, Rev. Wallace Heflin, Jr., traveled a lot in ministry, as I did, and sometimes we lacked time to share with each other the great things God was doing. Once, when I was coming from Israel and he had a group ready to fly out for another ministry trip, we met in the airport in Washington, D.C.

We talked as he checked his people in, as quickly as possible placing suitcases on the scales. He had only recently made his first trip into Russia since the country had opened for preaching, and I was anxious to know how his crusades had gone. "How was Russia?" I asked, in the midst of the confusion.

Tears came to his eyes as he replied, "If I had only been born for those two weeks, it would have been worth it all. They were the two greatest weeks of my life."

In one meeting, in just a few moments' time, fifty-eight deaf and dumb people had been healed. As I said, we have seen these things in other countries, but God is beginning to do great signs and wonders here in America as well. The river of God is flowing and wherever that river flows, it brings life.

Let the divine life of God flow through you. Don't do anything to hinder it. Give it free rein, for it is powerful.

My brother prayed for several people through the years who had metal pins in their legs and, afterward, X rays showed that no metal pins were any longer present. One man even had his knee frozen into an unmovable position through surgery, yet he was able to move it normally after prayer. These things are not difficult for our God, and wherever the river flows, similar things will happen.

> We are only just beginning to tap into the power of the river of God. In it is an endless supply of all the power we need.

A sister was at our campmeeting this past summer. My brother had prayed for her several years ago because she had no little finger. Now she has a beautiful "pinky" and she gives all the glory to God. In the river, anything is possible.

I am determined to live in the river and to know its divine flow, not only for my own life, but for the benefit of many others as well. For some, healing is still a difficult thing to believe for, but for God it is a small thing indeed. When you allow the river to flow over your soul and spirit with its healing waters, sickness and disease simply cannot remain in you. Wherever the river flows, everything in its path will be healed.

Don't fail to be used of God in this healing revival, as He reaches out to countless men and women all over the world in this last day and hour.

Around the world the power of many great rivers are harnessed by hydroelectric plants that create enough electric current to power the factories and homes and businesses of great cities. We are only just beginning to tap into the power of the river of God. In it is an endless supply of all the power we need. Get into the river and experience *River Glory* now.

Chapter 5

Our Guide in the River

*Afterward HE BROUGHT ME again unto the
door of the house. ... THEN BROUGHT HE
ME out of the way of the gate northward, AND
LED ME about the way without ... and HE
BROUGHT ME through the waters. ... Again
HE ... BROUGHT ME through the waters. ...
Again HE ... BROUGHT ME through.*
Ezekiel 47:1-4

"He brought me ... and led me." We have a divine
Guide who will take us through these waters.

In this realm of the Spirit, in the mighty flow of
the river of God, there are areas that we could never
hope to know on our own. In the vastness of this
river, we could easily and quickly be lost and not
even know where we were or which way to turn.
We need to be led, and God has provided us with a
most wonderful Guide, the Spirit of God Himself.

As we have seen, the vastness of the river frightens some. To them it is unknowable and, therefore, to be feared. God is not sending us into the river alone, however. He has given us a Guide. The same person who served as Guide to Ezekiel as he entered the waters was also described by him in an earlier chapter:

> *In the five and twentieth year of our captivity, in the beginning of the year, in the tenth day of the month, in the fourteenth year after that the city was smitten, in the selfsame day the hand of the LORD was upon me, and BROUGHT ME THITHER. In the visions of God BROUGHT HE ME into the land of Israel, and set me upon a very high mountain, by which was as the frame of a city on the south. And HE BROUGHT ME THITHER, and, behold, there was a man, whose appearance was like the appearance of brass, with a line of flax in his hand, and a measuring reed; and he stood in the gate.*
>
> Ezekiel 40:1-3

"*And he brought me thither.*" Oh, I like that. There are places that you and I long to go spiritually. We have read about them in the Scriptures. We have read about what happened to Ezekiel and Zechariah and others of the prophets when they went there. We long to flow into these new places in God, for they seem to be just at our fingertip, just across the threshold.

Still, we are not quite sure what we need to do in order to enter these new areas, what direction to take to press forward into the fullness of what God has prepared. The deeper things of God seem so elusive to us, and we wonder how we, too, can know the place of greater intimacy with God, the place of revelation in His Spirit.

I am so glad that the Teacher, the Guide, is among us. We need not hang back any longer. The Spirit of the Lord is ready to take us forth into the unknown and make it known to us. He is our river Guide.

> How do you reap a worldwide harvest? How do you organize a worldwide revival? We don't have to worry about it. The Guide, the Teacher is with us.

Where is the place of wisdom? Where is the place of understanding? We don't have to worry about it, for He will bring us there: *"He brought me thither."* He brought me to the place of revelation, the place of understanding, the place of wisdom, the place of the unfolding of knowledge.

How do you reap a worldwide harvest? How do you organize a worldwide revival? We don't have to worry about it. The Guide, the Teacher, is with us.

The fact that He is our Guide explains the great hunger within us to know the Lord better. When two people are attracted to each other, they want to get to know one another. They can never be satisfied with a superficial introduction: "Tom, meet Mary. Mary, meet Tom." Oh no, there is a desire for much more.

It may be a while before they feel as if they know each other well enough to ask personal questions, so they ask a friend (as subtly as possible), "What do you know about him?" "What do you know about her?" Yet, no matter what they are told, it is never enough. They keep asking questions: "Well, did he say this?" or "Does he like that?" or "Is she ... ?" The desire to know is so great that it seems unending. Once you know something about someone to whom you are attracted, you want to know it in more detail.

When the two have finally begun to ask things of each other, their desire to know accelerates until they find themselves asking and answering questions that nobody was ever interested in before. They find themselves having to pull memories from the deep recesses of their hearts. The desire to know is just that powerful.

God's desire is to take us places we can't ask to be taken because we don't know they even exist. He wants to give us experiences that we could never request because we have never yet even dreamed of them.

God is birthing within us much more than the superficial hunger many of us have had until now to know Him. In the days ahead, we will want to know details that nobody has been able to tell us about Him until now. We will no longer be satisfied with cold information about Him. Only living knowledge, revealed from His very heart, will suffice, only the passing of glory from His heart to ours.

If we are to allow our Guide to bring us *"thither,"* we will need to lay aside our reasoning minds and allow Him to carry us away as He wills. Some of us are so busy telling Him where to take us and how to do it that we miss the greater things He has to show us in the river. We are so need oriented that while He is trying to take us into new places and teach us new things, we are busy explaining to Him our problems and the situations we perceive as needing His touch. God's desire is to take us places we can't ask to be taken because we don't know they even exist. He wants to give us experiences that we could never request because we have never yet even dreamed of them. It is so much better to relax and let the Guide show you what is wonderful and worth seeing. He knows where the greatest treasures are hidden.

When you are in the presence of God, resist the temptation to think about your plans for tomorrow, next week or next year. Live in the moment, that eternal moment in God.

When God is beginning to lift you up, don't suddenly remember what you have to do tomorrow. The enemy likes to bring to us these diversionary thoughts, but we must learn to resist them. When you are in the presence of God, resist the temptation to think about your plans for tomorrow, next week or next year. Live in the moment, that eternal moment in God. Don't expect Him to show you what you want; let Him show you what He wants. He is the Guide.

Don't expect Him to show you what you want; let Him show you what He wants. He is the Guide.

I love to hear people share the visions they are having because as I listen to them I begin to get a sense of where the Holy Spirit is taking them and what He is doing new in their lives. He is our Guide for the river.

We need to be guided more than we know, for this river, as far as our natural minds are concerned, is totally uncharted. There is no preacher in the world who knows the whole river, yet we know Someone who does. *"He brought me thither."* Praise God!

What was the one like who was guiding Ezekiel? He said:

> *Behold, there was a man, whose appearance was like the appearance of brass, with a line of flax in his hand, and a measuring reed; and he stood in the gate.*   Ezekiel 40:3

He is the same man that Ezekiel saw in chapter 47, the man who led him out into the river and measured it for him. His appearance is *"like the appearance of brass."* Calm all your fears, and follow Him into the depths of the river, for He is the Lord of glory.

Why should we be afraid? Although "new" and "change" are not words that most of us like and represent a fearful thing for most people, our Guide knows what we can handle. He is capable of measuring, of knowing our ability, of knowing how far we are able to go. He will not thrust us suddenly in over our heads and leave us to drown. He will measure and lead us a little deeper, as we are ready and willing.

There are ever-greater depths for us to explore, but the Spirit Himself goes with us and is the One to measure everything for us. There is no reason for fear.

There are ever-greater depths for us to explore, but the Spirit Himself goes with us and is the One to measure everything for us. There is no reason for fear.

One of the greatest hindrances to revival is the fear that grips religious leaders when confronted with the new. They are so well trained that when something falls outside their religious training, they try to avoid it. Leaders are often the last to move into revival. They almost have to be dragged, kicking and screaming, into it. What a shame!

What are we afraid of? This river is of God and He Himself is our Guide.

Oh, I want to know Him. I want to know Him in ways that I have not known Him until now. I want to trust Him implicitly with my life and allow Him to be my Guide in the river.

The tides of spiritual hunger are rising all over America and the world. As I said, many hungry people are traveling long distances to come to Ashland, Virginia, to our humble open-air tabernacle in the woods. They are not drawn by luxurious accommodations or the hope of finding a nice place to spend a vacation. They spend time, money and effort to get to a place where the river is flowing and where they can get to know the Guide better and learn to follow Him. These are busy people, but they know that there is nothing more important in this day and hour than getting in the flow of what God is doing. How about you? Are you getting into *River Glory*?

Part II:

The Benefits of the River

Chapter 6

Revival in the River

And by the river upon the bank thereof, on this side and on that side, shall grow all trees for meat, whose leaf shall not fade, neither shall the fruit thereof be consumed: IT SHALL BRING FORTH NEW FRUIT ACCORDING TO HIS MONTHS, because their waters they issued out of the sanctuary: and the fruit thereof shall be for meat, and the leaf thereof for medicine.

Ezekiel 47:12

"*It shall bring forth new fruit according to his months.*" There is revival in the river of God.

The book of Revelation confirms the presence of the trees Ezekiel saw and their leaves and their healing powers. God is intent upon healing the nations, and in the days ahead, we will see national and international revivals.

Those who have never been to other countries need to get their traveling shoes ready and their suitcases packed. At some point in this revival God will give many the privilege of standing on foreign soil to help gather in the harvest from among the nations.

This, however, is America's time for revival. I spent forty years of my life overseas, but I knew shortly before my brother died, on December 27, 1996, that I was coming back to America. It had nothing to do with his death. The Lord had trained us as pioneers of revival, and I sensed that we would be needed in America. I can't remember a single country we ever went to that did not experience a move of God.

Those who have never been to other countries need to get their traveling shoes ready and their suitcases packed. At some point in this revival God will give many the privilege of standing on foreign soil to help gather in the harvest from among the nations.

I have heard it said that revival rarely lasts for

more than three to five years and never more than eight years, but I cannot remember a time in my life when I wasn't living in revival. I began fervently serving the Lord at about thirteen and after I committed my life to the nations, God gave me opportunity in one country after another to help bring forth His revival.

Still, I believe that we are living in a unique time. We are privileged to be part of the last-day ingathering, and we should not expect anything but success. Timing is on our side. This is the moment on God's timetable when we will see the ingathering of the greatest harvest, not only across America but all around the world.

As revival came at the beginning of the twentieth century, the end of the century will also know revival. The year 1999 will be a major revival year. Where there is no revival, it will break forth, and where it already exists, it will increase and accelerate.

When I decided to come back to America, some of my friends were concerned that I was losing my vision for the rest of the world, but shortly after my brother died and we were having our yearly ministers' conference, the Lord told me, "I will show you the pattern." What I saw suddenly was the hand of God dropping out of Heaven a wonderful blue gossamer fabric, and on it I saw the outline of America.

Lights began to come on all across this great nation until it was lit up with the very glory of God.

America is still the leader among nations, and God will use the people of America to bless other nations. He will use the finances of America to bring about the world harvest. Americans will have a special place in the harvest.

No nation and no denomination within individual nations will remain untouched by the revival. God will pour out His Spirit as we have never seen it before. I have seen the Lord in vision entering churches of all types. I have seen Him standing before churches with high altars and special lecterns, just as He stood in the synagogues of His day, and He opens the book and declares revival.

In the biblical record, we see Jesus declaring His will in the synagogue in Nazareth:

> *And there was delivered unto him the book of the prophet Esaias. And when he had opened the book, he found the place where it was written, The Spirit of the Lord is upon me, because he hath anointed me to preach the gospel to the poor; he hath sent me to heal the brokenhearted, to preach deliverance to the captives, and recovering of sight to the blind, to set at liberty them that are bruised, To preach the acceptable year of the Lord. And he closed the book, and*

*he gave it again to the minister, and sat down.
And the eyes of all them that were in the synagogue were fastened on him. And he began to
say unto them, This day is this scripture ful-
filled in your ears.*   Luke 4:17-21

The Lord is appearing, even now, in this same
way, in churches throughout the world, and He is
declaring what will soon be.

If we had to worry about bringing revival ourselves, it would be an overwhelming thought. We
have supernatural help in this revival. You and I
would not know how to begin. We would have no
idea how to organize and orchestrate the revival.
Even if we had all the necessary financial resources
at our disposal, we still could not make it happen. It
takes the presence of the Lord.

**No nation and no denomination
within individual nations will remain untouched by the revival. God
will pour out His Spirit as we have
never seen it before.**

I see Him standing at pulpit after pulpit. I see Him
visiting the Presbyterians. I see Him visiting the

Episcopalians. I see him visiting the Lutherans. I see Him visiting the Seventh Day Adventists. I see Him visiting the Baptists. I see a great visitation of God in all of the different Pentecostal denominations. I see the pastors of those churches lying flat on their faces, prostrate before God in the river. I see them throwing out their formalities. I see them throwing out their orders of worship. I see them throwing out their liturgies. I see countless numbers of people as they are bowing before God, prostrate on their faces, and the river of God is flowing over them.

This revival will go far beyond churches. Not a single government organization or department will be untouched by it. The river will seep in through every crack. There will be no way to keep it out of every government building.

I have seen God in vision going into our great Treasury Building on 14th Street in Washington, D.C. He is already at work in the Pentagon, the Congress and the Supreme Court buildings. He is already at work in the White House. We have seen Him moving into the Department of Transportation. I have even seen Him visiting the United Nations, and we will hear about His outpouring on one person after another.

Sometimes we are so disturbed by the activities of our U.S. and international institutions that we forget about the individuals who work there who love God. We have had many United Nations employees attending our meetings in Jerusalem. We are acquainted with one lovely gentlemen from Ghana who loves the Lord and is always in church on weekends, seeking God. When Secretary of the United Nations Kofi Annan was flying into Iraq for special negotiations to try to prevent another Gulf War, he chose this brother to go with him. There are many godly men and women working in government, here and abroad, and they will not be bypassed in this revival.

I have seen the Lord in vision personally visiting the individual governors' mansions across our nation. He is not leaving anyone out.

This revival will go far beyond churches. Not a single government organization or department will be untouched by it. The river will seep in through every crack. There will be no way to keep it out of every government building.

Since September of 1997 we have been having meetings every weekend in our camp in Virginia. We had never done this before, and it is very demanding on our time, but when the river is flowing, we must make room for it in our personal lives. We had to make ourselves available to the river, without thought for our own personal convenience.

As our summer campmeeting was closing that year, we announced that we would have the weekend meetings for a month to see what happened. People were coming from many parts of America and God was doing a wonderful work in their lives. After a month, we could not even think of closing our weekend meetings, and they have continued until this time.

In reality, we were not conducting the meetings for the people who were coming. We were doing it for ourselves. God had shown us that He wanted to move us into something deeper, take us into something higher. He did that, and we have all grown as a result.

Revival has shaken the small town of Smithton, Missouri (population 532). Pastor Steve Gray told me that he had felt like he was at the end of his rope as far as ministry was concerned. Things were not going as he wanted, so he decided to travel to Pensacola, Florida, to attend the Brownsville revival and to see what God would do for him. As he sat in the meetings, he realized that he had no idea what it was that God wanted him to do. He only knew that he had come to the end of himself.

"Go back to Smithton," the Lord told him, "and have revival."

"Lord, I can't do it," he protested and proceeded to give all the reasons why it couldn't happen.

"I didn't tell you to *be* the revival," the Lord answered him, "You are to *host* the revival." Pastor Gray was reluctant, but if the Lord was willing to do the work, how could he refuse?

He was not a demonstrative man. He had never danced in the Spirit nor leaped for joy, but when he returned to Smithton and stepped into his church, a spiritual lightning bolt from Heaven hit him and he began leaping and leaping and leaping. He had made contact with the river, and the river had connected with him. The revival in Smithton is ongoing and has captured the attention of the whole world. More people are attending that one church than live in the entire town.

> God always chooses the Bethlehems and the Nazareths of this world. He chooses the Smithtons and the Ashlands. It is because He does not want anyone to glorify the place rather than the river.

One well-known minister visited Smithton, and when he saw how small the town was and that it didn't even have a Coke machine, a gas station or a restaurant, he said he understood exactly why God had chosen that place for revival. "If God can send revival to Smithton," he said later, "none of the rest of us have an excuse not to have revival."

God always chooses the Bethlehems and the Nazareths of this world. He chooses the Smithtons and the Ashlands. It is because He does not want anyone to glorify the place rather than the river. He wants to be the focal point of the quest, so He chooses sights that no one would travel to for any other reason except to experience Him. God wants us to come to His river just for Himself. He is saying to us, "I am enough. I am all that you need." We have had far too many distractions. Concentrate on the river, and revival will come to you.

God wants to use you, and if you are willing to host revival, to let the river flow through your life, the Spirit of God will do the rest. You can't generate revival; only God can do that. If you are willing to get out of His way, however, and let the river flow, it will happen.

When the river is present and flowing, things happen quickly and easily. In both of my first books, *Glory* and *Revival Glory*, I mentioned that the Lord showed me in Jerusalem a number of years ago that when revival had broken out across America, Dallas, Texas would be the center of that revival. I told that on television in Dallas and also in other cities. Interestingly enough, until that time Dallas had been considered, in recent years, one of the hardest places in America to have a meeting. Those who were organizing conferences wanted to have them in other places because they feared they could not get a response from the Dallas public. God began to work in the lives of the people of Dallas and, before long, many conferences were being scheduled in Dallas because Dallas quickly got the reputation of being the easiest city in America in which to have revival and to conduct a conference.

Whenever God has sent me to any nation or city or town or village to declare revival, the people have always answered, "This place is different. The people here are hardened and unconcerned. This is the hardest place in the world to have revival." I listen, but then I begin to tell the miracles of what God did in the last place. The last place, before the miracles started, was also "the hardest place in the world." There are no hard places when the river is flowing. When revival breaks out the places that seem the hardest suddenly become easy. No matter how hard your town is or your church or family, begin to let the river flow in your life and it will sweep away every obstacle to revival. There is revival in the river. Get in and experience *River Glory* for yourself.

Chapter 7

Revelation in the River

And he said unto me, Son of man, HAST THOU SEEN THIS? Then he brought me, and caused me to return to the brink of the river.
Ezekiel 47:6

"Hast thou seen this?" There is a realm of divine revelation awaiting us in the river of God.

When the original disciples were filled with the Spirit on the Day of Pentecost, a new dimension came into their lives. Not only had they heard a sound from Heaven, *"as of a rushing mighty wind,"* not only had that sound *"filled all of the house where they were seated,"* not only had tongues of fire sat upon their heads, and not only had they all spoken in other tongues as the Spirit of the Lord gave them utterance, but this outpouring of the Holy Ghost brought many new dimensions to them. One of those new dimensions was in the realm of seeing.

75

Soon after Pentecost, Peter and John had an unusual experience. They had often gone to the Temple
to pray, and when they did, they had always passed
a lame man who customarily sat outside the gate. It
was not until they had experienced Pentecost, however, that they really noticed the man. They had
received healing ability long before this and had already been used in healing miracles many times, but
with Pentecost came a new ability in the realm of
seeing, an anointing to see what had gone unnoticed
before. This led to a new dimension in their healing
ministry as well.

> In the flow of the river of God, you
> experience a defining moment,
> catching a glimpse, often for the very
> first time, of the purpose of your life.

This same thing happened to Ezekiel. He was led
out into ankle-deep water, and he progressed into
knee-deep and loin-deep water, until finally he came
into waters in which he could swim. It was only then
that he was asked the amazing question, *"Have you
seen this?"*

When you are swimming and are surrounded by

water, what is there to see? Obviously there was something important to be seen or the Spirit would not have asked the prophet the question. There is a reason God takes us out into the depths of His glory, and that reason is to enlarge our vision, to make us capable of seeing more clearly into the eternal realms.

In the flow of the river of God, for example, you experience a defining moment, catching a glimpse, often for the very first time, of the purpose of your life. We were not intended to drift through life without meaning and purpose. There is a reason for our existence, and the river makes that reason plain. There are many things scattered about us that we have not yet noticed or we have not yet noticed enough. We may have had glimpses of them and limited understanding of their worth, but now, in the midst of the flowing of the river, everything suddenly becomes focused, and we see the meaning of the whole, the purpose for every part.

On the Day of Pentecost, when the many witnesses to the initial outpouring of the Holy Spirit were standing about dumbfounded, Peter was able to stand and say:

> *For these are not drunken, as ye suppose, seeing it is but the third hour of the day. But this is that which was spoken by the prophet Joel;*

*And it shall come to pass in the last days, saith
God, I will pour out of my Spirit upon all flesh:
and your sons and your daughters shall prophesy, and your young men shall see visions, and
your old men shall dream dreams: And on my
servants and on my handmaidens I will pour
out in those days of my Spirit; and they shall
prophesy: And I will show wonders in heaven
above, and signs in the earth beneath; blood,
and fire, and vapour of smoke: The sun shall be
turned into darkness, and the moon into blood,
before that great and notable day of the Lord
come: And it shall come to pass, that whoso-
ever shall call on the name of the Lord shall be
saved.*   Acts 2:15-21

Peter had read the prophecy of Joel many times,
but suddenly, from his new vantage point out in the
depths of the river, he began to see things that he
had never seen before. He suddenly became aware
of exactly what was happening to him and to those
around him and was able to relate it to prophecies
that had come forth hundreds of years before.

When Ezekiel first stepped into the waters, he had
not yet noticed the trees along its banks, and he had
not yet realized their potential for healing the nations. It was only after he was taken out into deeper
waters that he saw the trees and saw their powerful

leaves and knew what they were and what they could accomplish.

Surely God had wanted Ezekiel to see all this much earlier, but it is only as we move into the depths of the river that we begin to see what God has wanted us to see all along. Until that moment, it is all there, but it is not apparent to us. It is somehow hidden. It is only when the Spirit of God gives us clarity of vision that we can see what has always been there for us to see.

> Healing for the nations seems like a lofty goal, a difficult thing to believe for, but after Ezekiel had seen it with his own eyes, it was not only easy to believe for, but it also became easy for him to declare.

Healing for the nations seems like a lofty goal, a difficult thing to believe for, but after Ezekiel had seen it with his own eyes, it was not only easy to believe for, but it also became easy for him to declare. Seeing in the realm of the Spirit brings to us a new sense of ease in God.

When you have seen people you know in the Spirit and seen them doing exploits for God and reaching multitudes, they may be just as naughty as they always have been for a while, but you will know from that day forth that God already has His hook in their jaws. Their day is coming. God has a purpose for the lives of men, and when we catch a glimpse of it in the glory realm, we can believe for them to rise out of their worldliness and enter into God's plan for the ages.

Unless we allow the river of God to affect our seeing, we can accomplish little for His Kingdom.

"Have you seen this?" Well, probably not, but if we get into the river, we can.

Unless we can first see such things in the realm of the Spirit, we often will not be able to believe for them, and unless we allow the river of God to affect our seeing, we can accomplish little for His Kingdom.

This subject is so important that I often teach on it, and people sometimes ask me what I mean by "seeing." I am speaking of a seeing that is not with natural eyes, but with the eyes of the Spirit.

It is said of the Living Creatures that they were *"full of eyes round about"*:

And their whole body, and their backs, and their hands, and their wings, and the wheels, were full of eyes round about, even the wheels that they four had. Ezekiel 10:12

Those living creatures had eyes everywhere. Where can we locate the eyes we suddenly begin to use when we get into the river of God's glory? Only God knows. What I can say for sure is that when we come out of the river, we should have very different eyes. We should know the purposes of God and no longer be easily troubled by the events of life or by the responses of people.

God has some new things for you to see. If you had a vision twenty years ago that changed your life, but you haven't had a vision since, then God wants you to drink until you see new things. If vision is new to you, He wants you to be carried out in the Spirit until you begin to see what has been unnoticeable for you until now.

You may not have an amazing vision. Ezekiel just saw some trees. He knew, however, that those trees were for the healing of the nations. With the seeing came a spirit of revelation which dropped into his spirit the understanding of what the Lord was saying and doing.

Sometimes what we see in the Spirit can be quite simple. We somehow want to receive the whole book of Revelation before we are willing to admit that we see in the Spirit. When you get out into the depths of the river, however, and start drinking, you will find yourself looking with new eyes and seeing things you never imagined seeing.

You will look at people differently. You will see the revival differently. Your response will be a different response. It will be according to the seeing that God is putting into your spirit. May God do the work in each of us, allowing us to come into a deeper realm of revelation.

Many powerful passages of scripture reveal God's desire to take us into realms of seeing:

> *And when I saw him, I fell at his feet as dead. ... Write the things which thou hast seen, and the things which are, and the things which shall be hereafter.*   Revelation 1:17 and 19

> *Howbeit we speak wisdom among them that are perfect: yet not the wisdom of this world, nor of the princes of this world, that come to nought: But we speak the wisdom of God in a mystery, even the hidden wisdom, which God ordained before the world unto our glory: Which none of the princes of this world knew: for had they known it, they would not have crucified the Lord of glory. But as it is written, Eye hath not*

*seen, nor ear heard, neither have entered into
the heart of man, the things which God hath
prepared for them that love him. But God hath
revealed them unto us by his Spirit: for the
Spirit searcheth all things, yea, the deep things
of God.* 1 Corinthians 2:6-10

*For he that speaketh in an unknown tongue
speaketh not unto men, but unto God: for no
man understandeth him; howbeit in the spirit
he speaketh mysteries.* 1 Corinthians 14:2

**There has always been revelation in
the river of God, but we are about to
see a release of revelation beyond
anything we have known before. In
that greater revelatory realm, we
will see and speak the very mysteries of God.**

There has always been revelation in the river of
God, but we are about to see a release of revelation
beyond anything we have known before. In that
greater revelatory realm, we will see and speak the
very mysteries of God. That which we do not now
know, that which is not visible to the natural eye or

audible to the natural ear, and that which the natural heart cannot yet perceive will come to us by the revelation of the Holy Spirit.

I love the book of Revelation because in it we see the unfolding of revelation to the Apostle John. He was exiled to a remote island, and his circumstances were not at all good, but then suddenly he was carried away in the Spirit on the Lord's Day, and he began to see and hear things he had never seen or heard before.

When John saw the seven stars in the hand of the Lord, he had no understanding of what that might mean in the natural. When he saw the candelabra with the seven candlesticks, he had no understanding of what that might mean. As he proceeded in revelation, however, seeing the very visions of the Lord, the mysteries began to unfold before him, and he understood that the seven stars were the angels of the seven churches.

Pastors need to pay more attention to this passage. Many pastors feel isolated and alone. They feel that no one understands them. Pastors, you have a prophetic position in the very hand of the Lord. You are separated unto Him. You are one of those shining stars that John saw in his vision, and they were in God's hand.

When John saw the candlestick, he also saw the Lord in the midst of the candlestick, and he came to understand that the mystery of the candlestick is that it represents the seven churches.

God does not just give us similitudes and emblems, but He speaks to us in terms that we can understand. He didn't want John going around saying for the rest of his life, "I wonder what those stars were. That was a wonderful vision, and I'm glad I received it, but what could it mean?" When we surmise something we get ourselves in trouble. When we try to place our own interpretation on things, we often get more confused. *"The seven stars are ... and the seven candlesticks ... are ... ."* It is time to hear God speak clearly so that we might understand His mysteries.

I don't know about you, but I want to know the mysteries of God. This is a right given to us by God:

> *He answered and said unto them, Because it is given unto you to know the mysteries of the kingdom of heaven, but to them it is not given.*
> Matthew 13:11

So, if this is my right, something that has been *"given"* to me, I want to take advantage of it. Just as God spoke to John in words he understood, He will speak to me in ways that I also can understand.

When young people come in off the street into the Church, God doesn't speak to them in the English

of King James' time. He may even use some street
language to reveal to them His mysteries. He knows
how to express Himself to every one of us in unique
ways.

God has called us to be a people of
knowing. We should not always
have to wait so long to get His leading for every major decision.
Sometimes we don't have time for
another forty-day fast. It is time to
walk in the Spirit of revelation.

Once, when we were talking about the glory of
God in Jerusalem, a little boy raised his hand and
said, "I know what the glory looks like. It looks like
a great big marshmallow." I could tell that he had
indeed seen the glory, and it was not an unusual
way for a child to describe it. Someone a little older
might have said it looked like clouds, but to this boy
it was a great big marshmallow. God is revealing
Himself and showing us the mysteries of His Kingdom in ways that we can understand.

I'm hungry to know more and it is available to
us. As we learn to enter into the anointing — praising until the spirit of worship comes and worshiping

until the glory comes — we can stand in that realm of glory and receive revelation in the depth of the river of God, in its flow.

God has called us to be a people of knowing. We should not always have to wait so long to get His leading for every major decision. Sometimes we don't have time for another forty-day fast. It is time to walk in the Spirit of revelation. As we allow the Spirit to carry us out into the depths of the river, we will find ourselves knowing the next step to make and the timing of that next step, and it will all happen with ease as we come into new realms of the Spirit of God.

I hear men talking about their plans for revival these days, and their speech is filled with computer terms. God is going to do it differently than we imagine. He will do it with wind and fire and smoke.

When I hear about men's great harvest programs, most of them are so complicated that I never can get them all read. They are so complex they become wearisome. Get in some anointed meetings, and God will speak the simplicity of His harvest to your soul. It doesn't take God long.

I want to be a person who lives in that revelatory realm of the Holy Spirit, and nothing less will satisfy me. I trust that you feel the same way.

It is time to take up our *"watch"*:

*I will stand upon my watch, and set me upon
the tower, and will watch to see what he will
say unto me, and what I shall answer when I
am reproved. And the LORD answered me, and
said, Write the vision, and make it plain upon
tables, that he may run that readeth it. For the
vision is yet for an appointed time, but at the
end it shall speak, and not lie: though it tarry,
wait for it; because it will surely come, it will
not tarry. Behold, his soul which is lifted up is
not upright in him: but the just shall live by
his faith.*   Habakkuk 2:1-4

"*I will stand upon my watch and set me upon the tower,
and will watch to see what he will say unto me.*" There
is a whole revelatory realm that is just out there
waiting to be seen.

The eagle's face of the Living Creatures speaks of
that revelatory realm of the Spirit of God, the realm
of glory that God wants us to move into. We have
touched the fringes of it. We know it in measure,
but God wants to bring us into it in an immeasur-
able way. In the days to come we are going to move
into that realm of revelation by the Spirit.

We think we are the one initiating the thought,
but when the revelation comes, it comes from on
high. We haven't thought about it or even considered it. It is a thought that drops into our spirits

when we haven't had a pre-thought concerning it, when we haven't been thinking in that vein at all.

The Holy Spirit is the Initiator, He drops the thought into our spirit, and those holy thoughts that are dropped into our spirits are called revelations. They didn't emanate from us; they emanated from Him. They are the thoughts of the Lord at a given moment, the mind of Christ in action.

The Holy Spirit is the Initiator, He drops the thought into our spirit, and those holy thoughts that are dropped into our spirits are called revelations. They didn't emanate from us; they emanated from Him. They are the thoughts of the Lord at a given moment, the mind of Christ in action.

I know that positionally we say we have the mind of Christ, but when that revelatory realm comes it is not only doctrinally that we have the mind of Christ. It becomes a reality. The very thoughts of Christ begin to drop into our spirit, and they are active thoughts.

I firmly believe that unless we allow the Spirit of revelation to come to us, we will not be prepared for the things we will face in the last days of time. We will be taken by surprise again and again. The enemy will be able to "slip things over" on us and we will not be prepared for them in any way.

God wants us to be a prepared people, and our preparation must not be just a general preparation. Most of us are already prepared in that way. We must be prepared in the specific details of that which is coming so that nothing takes us by surprise. If we already have a whisper of the Spirit in our hearts and in our spirits, we will be able to make preparations for our families, for our churches, and for our communities. We can do it on a daily basis day with specific direction from the voice of the Spirit of God. We can get ready for that which is coming upon the face of the Earth.

God wants to anoint our eyes to see and our ears to hear, and to lift us into realms beyond anything we have yet experienced. God wants to send us such quickenings and such visions that we will lose all hesitancy and move forth with confidence. The urgency of the hour demands that we move quickly, not taking such a long time to respond to the voice of God. Let us be carried out into realms of knowing by the Spirit.

It will also be important in the days ahead not only to know by revelation but to implement what we know in the Spirit as well. Don't be guilty of trying to implement divine revelation with your own understanding. Begin in the Spirit and continue in the Spirit. Begin in the glory and finish in the glory. God's work will be done no other way.

Reason will lead you away from the divine purpose of God. Put reason aside and go with the flow of revelation in the river of God.

Stand in your assigned tower and watch to see what God will show you. Know the mind of Christ. Feel the heartbeat of the Father. Understand what He is doing before He even does it. If you are not a visionary, believe for it today and every day.

Stand in God's presence, praise until the spirit of worship comes, worship until the glory comes, then stand in His glory (or kneel or sit or lie in His glory) and look until you see what it is the Lord is revealing to you.

The fact that God showed John so many wonderful things lets me know that He wants to show Ruth those same things. He wants to show you too. He doesn't want us to remain ignorant of these things. His river is flowing so that He can reveal to us the mysteries that have been hidden from the foundation of the world. It is time for revelation.

Jesus spoke to His disciples in parables so that those who had no spiritual understanding could not comprehend what He was saying. Those who care nothing about the river or where it can take them will understand little or nothing of what we say here. Let those who are hungry for more of God have spiritual perception. Let revelation come to those who are thirsty for the move of God's Spirit. Get into the flow of *River Glory*.

Chapter 8

Promotion in the River

*Incline your ear, and come unto me: hear, and
your soul shall live; and I will make an ever-
lasting covenant with you, even the sure
mercies of David. Behold, I HAVE GIVEN
HIM FOR A WITNESS TO THE PEOPLE,
A LEADER AND COMMANDER TO THE
PEOPLE. Behold, THOU SHALT CALL A
NATION that thou knowest not, and NA-
TIONS THAT KNEW NOT THEE SHALL
RUN UNTO THEE because of the* LORD *thy
God, and for the Holy One of Israel; for he hath
glorified thee.*   Isaiah 55:3-5

"*I have given him ... to the people.*" God has a place
of promotion awaiting those who will step deeper
into His river. Nothing is more important in this period of end-time revival than the raising up of

leadership within the Church, and there is provision for it in the river.

In speaking of David, the Lord said that he was first called to be a *"witness"*, then he was promoted to *"leader"*, and finally he became a *"commander"* of the people.

We all share David's call to witness. Before He went back to Heaven, Jesus said:

> *But ye shall receive power, after that the Holy Ghost is come upon you: and ye shall be witnesses unto me both in Jerusalem, and in all Judaea, and in Samaria, and unto the uttermost part of the earth.*   Acts 1:8

Being a witness is more than testifying to others. We are called to be examples of the Gospel of Jesus Christ, of His salvation, of His keeping power, of the infilling of the Holy Spirit, of His healing, of His provision, of how He guides us, of how He works in our lives. We are witnesses to those around us, and our daily lives must speak forth the testimony of our God. If we expect others to get into the flow of the river, we must step down before them and show them the way.

There is much more to the Christian life, however, than being saved and filled with the Spirit. God wants to promote us, as He did David. The Scriptures declare:

> *For promotion cometh neither from the east, nor from the west, nor from the south. But God is the judge: he putteth down one, and setteth up another.* Psalm 75:6-7

Promotion in the Kingdom of God comes directly from the King Himself. The Lord has new positions for each of us, and because of the rapid growth in the Church, this is promotion time.

Promotion in the Kingdom of God comes directly from the King Himself. The Lord has new positions for each of us, and because of the rapid growth in the Church, this is promotion time. As we get into the flow of the river, we are enlarged and enabled to do what we could not do in ourselves.

"I have given him ... to the people." We are God's gifts of love to the world. It is a terrible thing when we meet people who were forty years old or older before anyone ever spoke to them about Christ. This is shameful and God is calling us to change it!

Why do we remain silent? Is it possible that our neighbors are "too sinful," "too educated," or "too rich" to be interested in the Gospel? I think not, yet we keep silence for these and a variety of other reasons.

New Christians are not nearly as guilty of this. They have a zeal for the lost and become a great blessing to the people in their community and those they work with. There is nothing more wonderful to them than to win someone to Christ. More of us need this fresh attitude. For some reason, we seem to find it easier to talk about the weather, about what we read in the newspaper, about the politics of the day or about almost anything than to talk about Jesus and His love.

Dog lovers seem to always know how to turn a conversation to their favorite interest. Sports fanatics are good at it too. Why can't we be like that? If the person we are with starts talking about the weather, we should be able to turn the conversation to Jesus. He controls the weather. If the person we are talking with wants to discuss the news, we should be able to bring Jesus into the picture. He is behind all the world's events. If people insist on talking about their pets, tell them about your dog that was sick and you prayed and it was healed.

Some people say, "I have no gift in this regard." The truth is that you *are* the gift, and if you will be faithful to be a shining light to those around you, God will elevate you to other positions as well. Let the river enlarge your spirit and make you a man among men or a woman among women.

While you may insist that you have no gift of this calibre, you will never know until you get it unwrapped. That's the way gifts are.

While you may insist that you have no gift of this caliber, you will never know until you get it unwrapped. That's the way gifts are. You can keep them in beautiful boxes or wrapped in beautiful paper if you want, but you will never know what you have unless you open the gift. Your gifts may be from the best stores in town, but until you open them you have no way of knowing how they might benefit your personal life and the lives of others around you. Let every gift be opened before you so that you can know what you have in God.

David was exalted by progression, but every promotion was related to a ministry to people. Some of us want spiritual positions that don't include dealing with people, but there are none. Every spiritual position is directly connected with people. When you get to the place that you want nothing to do with people, you are not letting your spiritual gift flow. Promotion requires that we feel the heart of God and His heart is toward people.

I have known preachers who loved to preach, but hated people. How can that be? What are we doing in the ministry if not to serve people? A ministry that does not connect with people is meaningless. Ask God to give you a love for people as you float in the river of His power.

When we have witnessed to people, we become more concerned about their spiritual progress. Their care is not only the responsibility of pastors and teachers, but of every mature believer. If you will accept God's call to greatness, He will promote you today.

My brother seldom gave formal titles to those who worked with him. He loved it when people saw a need and got busy filling that need. He was thrilled when people didn't have to be asked or appointed, when they just felt the burden and acted. Those were the people he recognized as genuine leaders.

It is God who gives out leadership positions, but He does it in response to our willingness to see the need and step into it. If you are willing, He has many important positions to fill in His Kingdom. Step up and receive your promotion.

David moved up from leading to commanding.

God wants to give us a revelation of His plans and an authority to carry them out that will enable us to command others.

The centurion understood command, for he was a man under the authority of others and he had soldiers under his own authority. "Just speak the word," he told Jesus (see Matthew 8:8-9). May God give us more men and women like that centurion today.

Some insist, "I don't want anybody commanding me." Those who say this must not want to be in the last-day move of God. Every person who wants to be in this revival will become willing to have someone over them, raised up by God to command them in the flow of the river. Not everyone has climbed high enough on the tower to see clearly the course of the river. Some are still trying to decide if they even want to get in. Those who have climbed higher have chosen for themselves the gift of leadership. They are lifesavers for the rest of God's people. They can see the direction the river is taking and can point others in that direction.

David was given as a witness, and so are you. David was given as a leader and so are you. David was given as a commander, and so are you. It is time for you to take your rightful place in the river.

After showing the progression of David's calling, God showed Isaiah an even greater step in promotion:

> *Behold, thou shalt call a nation that thou*
> *knowest not, and nations that knew not thee*
> *shall run unto thee because of the* LORD *thy God,*
> *and for the Holy One of Israel; for he hath glo-*
> *rified thee.*   Isaiah 55:5

When we are willing to flow with the river of God, His Spirit will so indwell us that we are able to call people from afar. We don't have to be in India to call the Indians. We don't have to be in Africa to call the Africans. We don't have to be in the Islands to call the Islanders. We can stand in the place where God has put us in the depths of the river and receive a gift of the Spirit that will *"call a nation."*

We can stand in the place God has put us in the depths of the river and receive a gift of the Spirit that will *"call a nation."*

Some may say, "But my faith is not that big yet." That is why the Spirit of God wants to work in your life. If you are just a witness, let Him make you a leader. If you are just a leader, let Him make you a commander. If you are already a commander, reach out to greater things. Start calling nations unto the Lord.

Get ready. Promotion is coming to YOU. It may not happen as you might expect it to. No one will tap you on the shoulder and tell you that you have been promoted. You must take hold of the necessary authority in the realm of the Spirit. Don't wait for someone to prophesy your promotion. Take hold of it yourself. Say to the Lord, "Lord, I have been happy to serve You in this way, but I am ready for promotion. I want to have an authority that will enable me to reach out with my voice and call whole nations." God will honor your desire.

Someone might ask, "What good would that do?" When we are flowing in the river of God, our words are filled with Spirit and life, and we are capable of awakening nations for the Lord.

Some of our people have seen visions of revival further breaking out in our campground and they have seen Japanese and Chinese and people from other Asian countries and the world being drawn there because of the work of the Spirit. What God does in the days ahead will amaze us all. He said:

> *For my thoughts are not your thoughts, neither are your ways my ways.*   Isaiah 55:8

I don't know exactly how God will do it, but I have determined to be just as mindless in my ability to respond to Him as our Secret Service is to respond to the needs of our president. I don't want to always have to go through the phase of rationalization with my mind. I want to be so in tune with the Spirit of God and so in tune with what He is doing and how He is moving and working and flowing in this day and hour, that there will be in me an instant, spontaneous response.

The river doesn't wait for anybody. When something is flowing downstream and we want to catch it, we have to act fast or we may miss it.

When we are learning a foreign language, at the beginning we translate everything from English into the new language and from that language into English. When we, at last, have a full grasp of the new language, we think directly in that language, without having to translate everything back into our original tongue. This is the way the mature flow of the Spirit of God should work in our lives.

May we no longer consider the consequences of our actions nor weigh every move to be sure that we are not missing God's will. If we wait too long to move, we have already missed it because that part of the river has already moved on.

The river doesn't wait for anybody. When something is flowing downstream and we want to catch it, we have to act fast or we may miss it. It is easy to miss something being carried by a swift-moving current. The river is moving. Move with it. Step into your promotion today.

Some of us have gotten caught up in titles and, because of it, we have gotten locked out of other things God has wanted us to do. I have not been one to give titles because God is continually calling each of us to greater things. Don't let anyone limit your calling in God, rather let God take all limiting labels off of your life.

There is promotion in the powerful waters of God's flowing river. There is leadership ability just waiting for you. Every gifting and ministry is available there. Let the river flow through you, and promotion will come to your soul, the promotion of the Lord which is found in abundance in *River Glory*.

Chapter 9

Calling in the River

Then the word of the LORD came unto me, saying, Before I formed thee in the belly I knew thee; and before thou camest forth out of the womb I sanctified thee, and I ORDAINED THEE A PROPHET UNTO THE NATIONS. Then said I, Ah, Lord GOD! behold, I cannot speak: for I am a child. But the LORD said unto me, Say not, I am a child: for thou shalt go to all that I shall send thee, and whatsoever I command thee thou shalt speak. Be not afraid of their faces: for I am with thee to deliver thee, saith the LORD. Then the LORD put forth his hand, and touched my mouth. And the LORD said unto me, Behold, I have put my words in thy mouth. See, I have this day set thee over the nations and over the kingdoms, to root out, and to pull down, and to destroy, and to throw down, to build, and to plant. Jeremiah 1:4-10*

"I ordained thee a prophet unto the nations." For those who step boldly into God's waters, a worldwide calling awaits.

One of the greatest things that happens to us as we allow ourselves to be carried away in God's river is that we suddenly begin to feel His heart, to understand His ways. We suddenly have a burden for people, a calling to the nations.

> **For those who step boldly into God's waters, a worldwide calling awaits.**

I personally believe that there is no "local call." I hear people say, "We have a local call, a local ministry, a local vision," but I believe that every ministry is global. The Great Commission makes it so. When you go into the world and preach the Gospel to *"every creature"* you encounter, you may indeed find yourself based in a certain locality. My parents were in Richmond, Virginia for about sixty years, but although much of their work was local, their call and their vision was global.

The vision of every believer must always be for the whole world, and whether you ever physically go to foreign nations or not, it is essential that you have this dimension to the call of God in your heart.

Because of our human limitations, it requires a miracle for us to even contain God's vision. In the flow of the river, He gives us an enlargement of heart that enables us to carry the vision that He has placed within us. Rise to the occasion. It is time that we stop leaning always toward the lesser and begin to lean toward the greater. Rather than believe for the minimum, let us begin to believe for the maximum.

Because of our human limitations, it requires a miracle for us to even contain God's vision. In the flow of the river, He gives us an enlargement of heart that enables us to carry the vision that He has placed within us. Rise to the occasion.

When you get into anointed meetings where the river is flowing, the Spirit of God implants greatness into your spirit. He places a special calling within you, revealing the very reason you were born. To Jeremiah, He said, "Even from your mother's womb, you were called to be a prophet unto the nations." Your calling is no less dramatic.

Like us, immediately Jeremiah began to protest: "I am a child." The enemy will always put into our mouths something that has the power to minimize the call of God. If we insist on speaking these limiting thoughts, we may miss what God has for us.

The Lord said to Jeremiah (and He says to us today), "Don't even say it." If negative thoughts come into your spirit, resist them. Don't declare what you are thinking. Don't speak it out. Don't spend your time thinking on those negatives aspects, the "why it can't be me's."

Several years ago I flew into Vancouver, British Columbia, to speak in a Chinese church. Since my original call was to the Chinese people, they remain my first love to this day. When I got to the church that night, the Lord spoke to me and told me not to mention the word "Chinese." I protested, "Lord, You know I love the Chinese people, and I wouldn't say anything to hurt them." If I had said anything, I would only have mentioned that I was happy to be with the Chinese people again.

The Lord said, "I don't want you to put any limiting label on them. I am going to use them to bless the world, not just their own people." In the flow of the river, there is a high calling and every limitation that men would try to put upon us is taken away.

Many years ago my brother began inviting foreign pastors to our campmeetings, and we have continued that tradition. It requires a lot of effort.

Those who are in charge of this ministry send out several thousand invitation letters each camptime. Two copies of each letter must go out, one to the individual we are inviting and another to our Immigration Department. It has gotten more and more difficult for the people of the underdeveloped countries to get into America, but we love to bless those who would not ordinarily get an opportunity to come.

> In the flow of the river, there is promotion. Every limitation that men would try to put upon us is taken away.

Some can't understand why we make this effort. "There is plenty of work for them to do in India or Africa," they say. "Why should we invite them to come here?" Because the Great Commission is not just for Americans or Canadians or the British. Every believer needs to have a worldwide vision. Otherwise how can we expect our Lord to spend eternity with us? The world is His consuming passion, and He wants a people who have the world in their heart as well.

In the course of a year, we have people from more

than fifty countries who visit us here in Virginia, and in Jerusalem the number of nations represented in our meetings is more than one hundred each year. I am believing God for an increase in this number because I want to see His Word fulfilled. I know that when pastors and other Christian leaders from other countries get into the flow of God's river, their lives are turned upside down and they go back to their own countries to do great exploits for God.

Why should any believer be limited? God's call is all-encompassing.

The devil knows at least a thousand reasons he can present to each of us about why it can't be us that God will use. If he doesn't know all the why nots, our friends seem to know them. I personally believe that the call of God and the individual relationship of a person to his God is sufficient to cause it to come to pass in that person's life if he wants it and is willing to run hard after it. If you are decided, no man or devil can stop you or hinder you.

When we are willing to take hold of the vision of the Lord, it is amazing how God opens doors for us, doors that no man can shut. This has nothing to do with where we were born, our educational attainment (or lack of it), our social standing, or any of the other things that men consider to be so important. The important thing is one's individual relationship with God and the personal desire to believe and obey the Lord. This is what ultimately counts. Get into the river, and flow with its calling.

When we are willing to take hold of the vision of the Lord, it is amazing how God opens doors for us, doors that no man can shut.

Everything that has happened to each of us until this moment has been but a preparation for what we will move into in the days just ahead. We are experiencing more and more revival, and everything that we have experienced in the past — no matter how great the miracle or how wonderful the answer to prayer — has been but the earnest of the promise that we have been given for this last day and hour.

I was blessed because I was raised in a family that knew the glory of God. I can't remember a time when we didn't know the glory. I grew up in that realm of the glory and it is in the realm of glory that God plants seeds of greatness in our spirits. Let's stop talking ourselves out of the greatness God has prepared for us. He told Jeremiah not to say that he was a child, and He is telling you today to stop dwelling on the negatives and to accept His call and the greatness of it. Don't say anything that is limiting concerning yourself, concerning your ministry, concerning your calling, concerning what God has for you. Stop declaring limitations and start declaring the unlimited purposes of God. Start believing the burden of the heart of God — no matter what the existing circumstances. When you do, you will see great and supernatural doors opened to you.

> There is no limitation in the Spirit. There is no limitation in the glory. Those who dwell on the positive and confess the positive will be raised up overnight with special anointings that will amaze and confound the world.

My father had a great miracle ministry, and he said that God spoke to him these words: "I don't want you to speak a word of unbelief or to agree with others who do." He had to begin to cultivate this ability because if we are not careful we find ourselves, just in the course of normal conversation, speaking words of unbelief. After he had worked at this for a while and thought he was doing pretty well, the Lord spoke to him again: "It is not enough for you not to speak unbelief. I don't want you to even think it." From that day on, my father had to start the process all over again.

Get rid of some of the negative things you think and say. When you think like that and talk like that, you become your own worst enemy. Stop dwelling on and declaring the negatives and the limitations. There is no limitation in the Spirit. There is no limitation in the glory. Those who dwell on the positive and confess the positive will be raised up overnight with special anointings that will amaze and confound the world. What a wonderful day in which to live!

How long do you have to wait for some of these things to happen? If you will believe for it and stop insisting on the reasons it cannot happen, God will raise you up in a matter of months.

"But I'm not Jeremiah," I hear someone saying. There is an anointing for this day that is greater than Jeremiah's day. There is an anointing for this day that is greater than Isaiah's day. There is an anointing for this day and hour that is as great as anything that has ever been seen on the face of the Earth.

"What about the Day of Pentecost?" What about it? It is true that one hundred and twenty were filled with the Holy Spirit, but I have been in services in which thousands have been filled with the Spirit in one meeting, in a few minutes time. There has never been a greater day, a greater hour or a greater move of the Spirit of the living God. Begin to declare it. Accept your great calling in the river of God.

Why do we find it so hard to believe what God is telling us for ourselves? Once, when we were having Bible School every afternoon in Jerusalem, one of our leaders said to all the students, "I want you to go home tonight and write down any outstanding prophecy or vision or dream, anything that has not yet been fulfilled in your life and bring it back on a piece of paper tomorrow to class." When we got to class that next day everybody seemed to have done their homework, but they were embarrassed to show it. The papers remained hidden under something else, and the students didn't want anybody else to see or to know what they were anticipating in God. They didn't want anyone to think of them as being high minded, and they didn't want anyone to make fun of them.

The teacher went around the room, trying to get someone to read their paper first. Finally she got one of the students to reluctantly start reading off some of the things God had promised him. It said, "I am going to be a great evangelist. I am going to preach to thousands. I am going to see thousands saved." He was visibly embarrassed by what he had read.

The teacher, however, only encouraged him. "I don't see any problem with that," she said. "You are already preaching, you are already having success, you are already winning souls. The seed is already working. All God has to do for you is multiply the numbers, and that's an easy thing for God."

Another person read, "God has shown me that I would be preaching on large platforms in Africa, in great healing meetings, with great miracles."

"That's not difficult for God," the teacher responded. "Remember the lady you prayed for the other day. God healed her. What a miracle that was! Remember ...? " and she went on to remind him of other miracles God had done through him. The healing power was there. It just needed an acceleration, a multiplication in numbers. If God could heal one person through him, He could heal ten thousand people through him. Before we had finished that day, many were convinced that God would do what He had promised. We will see it in the days just ahead of us.

You are called to the nations. You perhaps have never thought of it in that way, but it is time you did. Get a good world map and pray over it. Lay your hands on the countries God burdens you for and believe for miracles. If you are not good at geography and don't know the countries, begin by praying for geographical areas or for continents. Pray for Asia, for Africa, for South and Central America. Pray for the Caribbean Islands. See what

God will do for you. This is God's day and hour to bring to fruition the call that has been on your life from your mother's womb. It is nurtured and enlarged as you are carried away in the river.

Some might say, "You don't know the kind of childhood I had." It doesn't matter. The call of God is not dependent on the family in which you were raised or even whether or not you were raised in a churchgoing family. God has an individual relationship with each of us that goes back to the moment we were formed in our mother's womb. His call is individual and personal.

The world is not too big for us to love. Move into your authority in God and begin to call forth nations for Him.

Just a couple weeks before my brother died, the Lord honored me and gave me the privilege of being in North Korea, the very last country I had been believing Him to send me to. I am blessed to have been in nation after nation, some of them for long periods of time and some of them over and over again. There must have been more than two hundred. This should not surprise us. It is what God promised. Get in the river, and it will happen in your life too.

Some people sit down and try to plan it, and while they are busy with the details of how they will get it done, God has already used the person next to them to accomplish the goal. Stop trying to do His work on your own and be carried away by the river.

> Some people sit down and try to plan it, and while they are busy with the details of how they will get it done, God has already used the person next to them to accomplish the goal.

Many American Christians are totally pessimistic about the future of America. Let the Lord give you faith for this country. Let Him give you faith for this generation. Stop being so pessimistic. God is not limited by existing conditions. Don't allow yourself to conform to the current trends of thinking. Be different. Allow the Spirit of God to drop faith into your heart for revival for America.

When I have seen revival recently in vision, I saw that it would extend "from sea to shining sea" in this country and that no nation in the world would remain untouched by it. God is going to bless the people of this world that many of us consider the least likely to be blessed. Stop trying to figure it out and let it happen.

Revival will soon break out on Wall Street, in the Congress in Washington and at the White House.

That house will also be filled with revival glory. The twentieth century has witnessed revival from Azusa Street to Brownsville, but it will not stop there. As we have seen, it is moving on to Smithton, Missouri, to Ashland, Virginia, to Phoenix, Arizona, to Annapolis, Maryland, and it is moving on to your town. Accept the calling to the world that God wants to place deep within your heart today through His *River Glory*.

Chapter 10

Wisdom and Knowledge in the River

*WHENCE THEN COMETH WISDOM?
AND WHERE IS THE PLACE OF UNDER-
STANDING? Seeing it is hid from the eyes of
all living, and kept close from the fowls of the
air. Destruction and death say, We have heard
the fame thereof with our ears. GOD
UNDERSTANDETH THE WAY THEREOF,
AND HE KNOWETH THE PLACE
THEREOF. For he looketh to the ends of the
earth, and seeth under the whole heaven; To
make the weight for the winds; and he weigheth
the waters by measure. When he made a decree
for the rain, and a way for the lightning of the
thunder: Then did he see it, and declare it; he
prepared it, yea, and searched it out. And unto
man he said, Behold, the fear of the Lord, that
is wisdom; and to depart from evil is understanding.* Job 28:20-28

"God understandeth the way therof, and he knoweth the place therof." There is a treasure house of divine wisdom and knowledge to be found in the river of God's Spirit.

Our God is all-knowing and all-seeing. He not only understands the way, but He knows the place. As we learn to flow in His wonderful river, He adds to us wisdom from on high.

There is no need for us to search out the wisdom we require. God has already found it. There is no need for us to seek the right way. He already knows the way.

If there is anything we are conscious of needing in this day of the move of the Spirit of God it is the understanding of the way of God and the place of God. Only He knows it, and if we want to get tuned into His thoughts, we must get into the river with Him and flow with what He is doing.

There is no need for us to search out the wisdom we require. God has already found it. There is no need for us to seek the right way. He already knows the way, and He knows the place thereof, and I am so glad that He is imparting His wisdom to us through the river's flow.

There is a realm in which in a moment's time God can teach you and give you great peace concerning every situation of your life. He can drop the answer you are searching for into your spirit. He can feed you in such a way that you go from spiritual kindergarten into intimacy in just a short time. It is not difficult for Him, when we allow ourselves to be carried away in the Spirit. What might take you years in natural time can be accomplished very quickly in the realm of the Spirit.

If we want to know God's wisdom and to have His understanding and be equipped for this last day move of the Spirit of God, there is only one way to accomplish it. He knows the place of wisdom. Let Him carry you there.

Solomon wrote:

> *The fear of the LORD is the beginning of wisdom: and the knowledge of the holy is understanding.*   Proverbs 9:10

Our God is wisdom and understanding, and the more we know Him in the holy dimension of His glory, the greater our understanding will be for the reivival of these last days.

I was able to graduate early from high school, having skipped several grades. The Thanksgiving before my graduation, I was trying to decide which college I would attend. My personal desire was to go to Wheaton College, where my Uncle Bill had done some graduate work, but I wanted to know God's desire. We were having special meetings during the holiday weekend, and I was praying seriously, trying to find God's will on this matter.

> Our God is wisdom and understanding, and the more we know Him in this holy dimension of His glory, the greater our understanding will be for the revival of these last days.

A group of Bible school students from Georgia was with us, and one day while I was praying at the altar, the principal of the group came by to pray for me. He had no way of knowing what was on my mind, yet he began to prophesy: "Desire not earthly knowledge and earthly wisdom. If you will seek My face, I will give you My knowledge and My wisdom." With that one sentence, I knew that I would not be going to college. I would seek the face of the Lord and gain wisdom and knowledge from Him. I never questioned God about the matter again.

It has been amazing through the years to see the

wisdom God has given me supernaturally. When I first went out to Hong Kong, I was only eighteen, yet before long, the Lord opened a wonderful door of ministry for me with the Full Gospel Business Men there. My friend was the Far East Asian Director of that organization. Often, in the years that followed, I would find myself sitting with successful businessmen, most of them already millionaires, and they would be asking me questions related to business. I had been raised in a small town atmosphere in Virginia in the humble home of pastors, and I had never held more than fifty dollars in my hand at one time. The questions these men posed involved thousands and even millions of dollars. I kept reminding myself of the Lord's promise, and God was faithful to give me wisdom to answer them. The answer He gave me was always exactly what that individual needed.

Sometimes, when I was asked a question, it seemed as if I was looking on as someone else gave the answer. I was listening to myself answer, and I was hearing the answer for the first time, just like the person I was speaking to. I certainly could not take credit later for what was said. The wisdom of God covers the lack of experience and training of a young person and will help us at any age to excel.

Thousands of times through the years I have experienced this same thing, as the wisdom of God has come to me in the river. If we are only willing to get into the flow of His waters, He will show us things that we don't know. He will pour wisdom and knowledge into us, for He doesn't want us to be "in the dark." Nothing should take us by surprise as children of God. As I said, we should know what is happening in the Earth before the Earth knows it.

God has destined us to be the head and not the tail, to be successful in all the things He has called us to, and it will not happen because of human reasoning. He is ready to drop an answer into our spirits so that we do not walk in error.

This river is filled with wisdom and if you are found in its waters, God's wisdom will be found in you.

Sometimes we get wrong advice from those around us. If we are willing to come into the presence of God and be lifted up in the Spirit, He will drop something into our spirits that will correct the situation. He knows all things.

There are realms into which God desires to take us and we can only be equipped for these adventures through the miraculous provision of the river.

Do whatever you have to do to get into its waters. Go wherever you have to go. Let the river of God's wisdom flow freely in your life. Don't let anything prevent it. Drink in God's wisdom. Drink in His knowledge.

When we think about what we should say in a certain situation, more often than not nothing comes to us. When the moment arrives, however, and a word is suddenly dropped into our spirits and we are given the authority to speak it, we have to ask, "Where did that come from?" It is a result of the time we have spent floating in the river of God's wisdom and drinking of His presence.

While we are drinking and drinking, we may not be aware of how that particular drink will affect us. Keep drinking and soon you will see. This river is filled with wisdom, and if you are found in its waters, God's wisdom will be found in you.

We are the *"babes and sucklings"* the psalmist spoke of, but with God's wisdom poured into us, we can have *"perfect praise"* coming forth from our mouths.

The Lord can cause a child who has never heard of the word of knowledge to stand up and begin to use that gift and others. Nothing is impossible to Him, and He can do it through us too — if we get into the flow of the river. Lessons learned in the river are the easiest and quickest kind. They are the type of lessons that we feel motivated instantly to act

upon. There is great wisdom and knowledge awaiting you in the river of God.

One day, as I was in the Spirit, I found myself on
the bottom of the river, with the waters washing over
me. When I got up from the floor where I had been
slain in the Spirit, I sensed that all the words of God
had flowed over me. I could not have repeated a
word to you, yet there was a consciousness that all
the word of God had flowed over my soul and spirit.

Stop looking for "a word" when God wants to
make all His word pass over you. Stop looking for a
cup of blessing when He wants to give you the
whole river.

When God called Jeremiah and set him over nations and kingdoms, He placed His word in
Jeremiah's mouth. Jeremiah didn't necessarily have
a specific word for that moment, but all the word of
God was in him for the future. Every word that he
would ever prophesy was in the river.

When the word of God passed over me as I was
in the river, I knew that every word of God I needed
until He came had already been delivered to me. It
had been put in my soul, placed into the depths of
my spirit.

"How is that possible?" someone might ask. Well,
we seem to trust computers more than we trust God.
We put a program on the computer with its corre-
sponding information and we trust that all the

information we need is there. All we have to do is push the right buttons, and the information we require will pop up on the screen or be printed out to the printer. When I say that God can cause all of His word to pass over us in the river, some people just can't believe it, but it's there. It's in the river, and anytime we need it, God can make it all come to our spirits. Great wisdom and knowledge await you in *River Glory*.

Chapter 11

Greatness in the River

*Now the L*ORD *had said unto Abram, Get thee out of thy country, and from thy kindred, and from thy father's house, unto a land that I will show thee: AND I WILL MAKE OF THEE A GREAT NATION, AND I WILL BLESS THEE, AND MAKE THY NAME GREAT; AND THOU SHALT BE A BLESSING: And I will bless them that bless thee, and curse him that curseth thee: and in thee shall all families of the earth be blessed.*   Genesis 12:1-3

"And I will make of thee a great nation, and I will bless thee, and make thy name great; and thou shalt be a blessing." There is greatness in the river of God, and if we can learn to flow with the river, that greatness will be imparted into our spirits.

If there is one thing I have learned about the Holy Spirit, it is that we encounter greatness when we move into His realm. There is greatness in the life of the Spirit which can come to an individual in no other way. This greatness doesn't come by heredity, it doesn't come by education, and it doesn't come by achieving a certain level of social standing. It only comes by the Spirit of the Living God. The need to flow in the river of God's Spirit, therefore, cuts across every economic and social strata of society.

We are the seed of Abraham by faith, and we have a great heritage.

Whether our ancestors came over on the Mayflower or whether our being an American is the result of some of the more modern calls sent forth by God to other lands and peoples, we are all here because someone responded to the voice of the Holy Spirit to become part of a new and great nation.

We Americans all have a great heritage. Whether our ancestors came over on the Mayflower or whether our being an American is the result of some of the more modern calls sent forth by God to other lands and peoples, we are all here because someone responded to the voice of the Holy Spirit to become part of a new and great nation. The United States of America is not an accident of history. It is a response to the heartcry of God. Perhaps no nation in the world, other than Israel, has received the same call to greatness.

Not only are we called to greatness as a nation, but as individuals. Each person who was willing to leave family and home behind and to respond to the desire of the heart to worship God in liberty accepted a personal call to greatness.

In former centuries, these people came mostly from European nations, such as the British Isles, Germany, Holland and the Scandinavian countries, but today they come primarily from the former Soviet states, from Latin America, the Caribbean and Asia. Whether each American cares to recognize it or not, everyone that comes here does so because God has a divine destiny for America, and we are all, therefore, called to greatness.

It was not by chance that at the turn of the twentieth century there was an outpouring of the Holy Spirit at a little American mission on Azusa Street in Los Angeles, California. The revival that followed Azusa Street had to be named after the street because the church was not imposing enough. There was no denomination that one could call it after. It was not the revival of a single person or denomination. Some tag had to be placed on it, so Azusa Street stuck.

Several years ago, a group of us were coming home from ministry in Australia. We had a layover of some ten hours in Los Angeles, so we decided we would go and see the place where it all started. We first went to the great Angelus Temple where Aimee Semple McPherson had preached, and someone there gave us directions to Azusa Street. "You won't find much," they warned. "There's nothing left but a street sign."

We had a poor map and there were a lot of one-way streets, so after a while we thought of giving up the search. "Let's try once more," I encouraged and just about that time we saw the little sign, "Azusa Street." We got out and stood under the sign and had our picture taken.

> **If people could only realize that when they are slain in the Spirit they are falling into greatness, surely they would fall down more often.**

There was no monument, no great museum, just a street sign. Azusa Street. It became the name of an important revival. A small street was destined for greatness.

God's thoughts are all of greatness for His people. Unlike us, He doesn't have a single petty thought. We sometimes want to see people be blessed, but not too blessed. We wouldn't want them to be more blessed than us. We want them to succeed, but not too much. We wouldn't want them to pass us by. Such a thought has never crossed the heart and mind of God. The Spirit of God is greatness, and the river of God that is flowing in these days contains that greatness.

That's why I find it difficult to understand that some people don't want to fall down in the Spirit. If people could only realize that when they are slain in the Spirit they are falling into greatness, surely they would fall down more often.

One sister who attended our campmeetings admitted that she was a little hesitant about falling. She had done it before, but the Lord had sort of knocked her out when it happened, and the idea of just yielding to the Lord and lying down before Him just didn't seem right to her. The first time it happened to her in the campmeeting, she didn't feel much. The next time she fell out she wasn't conscious of feeling anything while she was on the floor, but when she stood up, she began to stagger a bit. Before long, however, she found that she was thinking differently. God was putting different thoughts into her spirit, and she became aware that it was happening because she was allowing herself to be carried away with the river.

Stop trying to imagine what God is doing for you, in you and with you. Can we not trust that there is greatness in the river of God?

God has promised to make of us a great people. This promise was not just for Abraham. The seeds that God is sowing in our lives go far beyond finances and good health. He has placed seeds of greatness in our spirits that in the days to come will reap a great and supernatural harvest.

That which is happening in our services is a transaction between Heaven and Earth.

There is something about attending greatly anointed meetings. Your soul benefits from just sitting there, whether you do anything else or not. In these anointings, in these stirrings in the glory, seeds of greatness are being dropped into your spirit, and you will find them growing until you can stand up in the fullness of what God has for you in this last day and hour.

Sometimes a seed is found that a bird has apparently picked up on one continent and dropped on another. If the fowls of the air can do that, what about the activity of angels in this day? What about the activity of the Holy Spirit in this day? That which is happening in our services is a transaction between Heaven and Earth. As we are sowing to the heavens, God is taking that which we sow and is bringing forth revival glory to the ends of the Earth. He says, *"I will make of you a great nation, and I will cause your name to be great."* Believe for it.

God has not only raised up America for this last day revival. He has used this nation to bring into being every type of modern technology to cause the Gospel to go forth to the ends of the Earth.

In November of 1997 I was in Greenville, Texas, just south of Dallas. In the service I suddenly began to see the multiplication of the voice. I saw satellite television, and I stood and began to declare it — although I had no way of knowing just how God would do it. A month or two later God made it possible for a friend of mine who has a television station in Dallas to go on satellite television across America, and soon he gave me the opportunity to multiply my voice by broadcasting from his station. In a single half-hour program on satellite television, we could reach more people than Abraham reached in a lifetime, more people than I had in all my travels (which cost many thousands of dollars in airline tickets and great physical effort). In a single half-hour program on television we could reach out in a way that we could not otherwise have done in a lifetime. What a wonderful day in which we live!

God is doing things much differently than we might have anticipated, and He has plans to use us to accomplish greater things than we have yet imagined. Stop trying to figure out how you will do it. This is a new day. God knows how to add to us and multiply us and divide us for His glory. Let Him flood you with His seeds of greatness.

God gave me a little chorus:

> *There are seeds of greatness in me.*
> *To make me what He wants me to be.*
> *More than I think, and more than I can see.*
> *There are seeds of greatness in me.*

There is a new flow of the Spirit of God, and He is searching for those who will be just as adventuresome as Abraham of old. Abraham had no precedent to follow. He was the first person to leave home and country and follow after the voice of God. He was the first man to start traveling toward a place without knowing where that place was. He went out expecting an inheritance, yet after he got to where he was going, there was no apparent inheritance awaiting him, other than an inheritance by faith.

God is calling us to have the faith of Abraham, to

move into the realm of the unknown, to move in the direction of that which we have not yet seen. We are not to do it, as Abraham did, on the back of a donkey or camel. We may not be called on to cross desert places. But, like Abraham, we will reach our promised land by learning to go with the flow of God's river. The greatest task we have before us is to learn to relax, to stop working, and to be carried by the anointed waters. There is greatness in its flow.

"How paradoxical," some might say, but the Apostle Paul taught this truth long ago:

> *Let us labour therefore to enter into that rest* ... .
> Hebrews 4:11

We *"labor"* to *"enter into rest."* Once you have entered God's rest, you can relax in the arms of His Spirit and be carried away in its greatness.

Let fireballs from the Holy Spirit roll forth from your hands to do the work. Let sparks of fire come forth from your mouth so that your words will be effective.

Stop struggling and let it happen. Let fireballs

from the Holy Spirit roll forth from your hands to do the work. Let sparks of fire come forth from your mouth so that your words will be effective. Let the glory of God be manifested and revealed. This is the day of the river of God, and there is greatness in that river.

I have watched it happen through the years. When people get into the river, they are suddenly dreaming great dreams, having great visions, and exploring glorious plans.

I have watched it happen through the years. When people get into the river, they are suddenly dreaming great dreams, having great visions, and exploring glorious plans. Before they got in the flow of the river, they had no plan and their vision was limited. They were concerned only with the few, only with caring for their own families. Suddenly God raised them up to do signs and wonders and exploits in His name. He dropped greatness into their spirits beyond anything they had been raised in. It is the work of the Spirit of God, and it happens in the flow of His river.

God is calling out a people who will rise up in obedience to follow after His voice, a people who will accept His vision of greatness, a people who will respond to His high calling. He has promised to raise us up as a nation and to cause our names to be great. He said through Peter:

> *But ye are a chosen generation, a royal priest-hood, an holy nation, a peculiar people; that ye should show forth the praises of him who hath called you out of darkness into his marvellous light:* 1 Peter 2:9

When any person is chosen to represent our nation in some way, that person's shoulders seem to rise several inches, and their head is held higher than normal. Representing the nation is a distinct honor. You and I, however, have an even higher calling. We are called to represent the God of the Universe. Rise to the level of greatness that call demands by immersing yourself in the flow of God's river.

When you are under the power of God, you may not be aware of the seeds of greatness God is implanting in your spirit. You may not perceive the changes God is making in your heart. You may not be aware of the great things He is doing for you at that very moment. But it will all become obvious in time.

There is greatness in the flow of the river and that greatness will affect your life for the future as you step deeper into *River Glory*.

Chapter 12

Finances in the River

And all that believed were together, and had all things common; and sold their possessions and goods, and PARTED THEM TO ALL MEN, AS EVERY MAN HAD NEED.

Acts 2:44-45

And with great power gave the apostles witness of the resurrection of the Lord Jesus: and great grace was upon them all. Neither was there any among them that lacked: for as many as were possessors of lands or houses sold them, and brought the prices of the things that were sold, and laid them down at the apostles' feet: and DISTRIBUTION WAS MADE UNTO EVERY MAN ACCORDING AS HE HAD NEED.

Acts 4:33-35

"Distribution was made unto every man according as he had need." There is an ample supply of all that we need in the river. Whatever brings us to the river, if we can all get into it, every need will be supplied.

This present revival will not only touch the soul. It will be an economic revival for God's people. We will not only get out of debt, but we will receive outstanding financial miracles for our every need. We must believe for it. This is God's desire for every one of us.

This present revival will not only touch the soul. It will be an economic revival for God's people. We will not only get out of debt, but we will receive outstanding financial miracles for our every need.

In the Body of Christ worldwide, a great majority need financial miracles, and those who don't can exercise faith for those who do. This is an area where Satan attacks many of God's people. He wants to hinder the flow of God's river in any way he can. We must allow the river of God to run through our companies, through our banks and through our personal finances, for God desires to free us from every hindrance to do His will in this day and hour.

When the financial market became shaky in the summer of 1998, God spoke to us that it was to the advantage of revival for Him to keep the market steady. He said that although there would be little shakings the market would remain stable for the sake of revival.

It takes additional finances for God's people to be able to go to visit centers of revival where God is moving. One needs to be able to take a few days off work to go to revivals, campmeetings and crusades. This requires economic stability.

God is requiring greater fiscal responsibility from His people. Living on the mission field these many years we have practiced living debt free with the exception of current living expenses. My parents were told by the Lord never to put a mortgage on the camp property in order to protect it as a refuge for God's people in the future. God wants to free us from such encumbrances.

Revival is very good for the local economy. Everyone prospers in the towns where God is moving. There is an overflow of blessing. The local merchants are blessed. The motels and restaurants are full and all modes of transportation are utilized.

As we move into revival, God is miraculously get-

ting His people out of debt. He wants to free us individually and also pay off the debts of our churches.
Getting out of debt is totally opposite from the current trend here in the United States and in many
other countries. The American people are being encouraged to roll their excessive credit-card debt over
into home-equity loans. This only places people
deeper into debt and may even jeopardize the security of their homes in the future. This is clearly not
God's will. This is not the time to build bigger barns
to store our goods and declare that we are *"in need
of nothing."* God wants to free His people so that we
can participate fully in revival. Begin to believe for
it today.

> **Those who lack will miraculously be
> given what they need to meet their
> financial obligations, and those who
> have surpluses will be called upon
> to place some of their surplus into the
> Kingdom.**

Revival is touching our hearts, our souls, our
hands and our feet, but it is also touching our pocket
books. It is touching our bank accounts. Those who

lack will miraculously be given what they need to meet their financial obligations, and those who have a surplus will be called upon to place some of their surplus into the Kingdom. As God did it for the emerging church of the first century, He is doing it again, so that His people will owe this world nothing. All that we require is to be found in *River Glory*.

Chapter 13

Unity in the River

And I turned to see the voice that spake with me. And being turned, I saw seven golden candlesticks; And in the midst of the seven candlesticks one like unto the Son of man, clothed with a garment down to the foot, and girt about the paps with a golden girdle. His head and his hairs were white like wool, as white as snow; and his eyes were as a flame of fire; And his feet like unto fine brass, as if they burned in a furnace; and HIS VOICE AS THE SOUND OF MANY WATERS. And he had in his right hand seven stars: and out of his mouth went a sharp twoedged sword: and his countenance was as the sun shineth in his strength.   Revelation 1:12-16

"His voice [was] as the sound of many waters." **There**

147

is supernatural unity to be found in the depths of God's river.

When John saw Jesus, this is the way he described His voice. This is important to us, because the Lord is causing the Bride to speak as the Bridegroom, to have a voice just like His. Since the voice of the Bridegroom is *"as the sound of many waters,"* ours must be a unified voice too, many voices joined as one.

This is not a day for exclusivity. This is not a day to maintain separations. God is removing them all. Labels are falling off. Barriers are coming down. Offenses are being forgotten.

There is only one river, and we all have to get into the same one, but this river has *"many waters."* As our many streams come together into one stream, the sound of all are merged into one great sound. Right now we are too often many sounds, but God wants to make us one. This is not a day for exclusivity. This is not a day to maintain separations. God is removing them all. Labels are falling off. Barriers are coming down. Offenses are being forgotten. The waters of this river must be one, despite the fact that they are many.

It is wonderfully refreshing to listen to the sound of rushing water. Something about it brings peace to the soul. It is the same in the Spirit realm. All the fruit of the Spirit can be heard in *"the sound of many waters"* coming forth from the Body of Christ today.

When we are all singing in the Spirit together, every voice is distinct. If you get close enough to any one person, you may hear their distinct sound, but the overall impression is of one great voice. Each person is singing individual words of their particular language in the Spirit, but the impression is of the whole, not of the parts.

When you listen to that great collective voice, there is no hint of discordance. One individual singer may, indeed, be somewhat off-key, but the whole collective voice, the flowing together, produces something of great beauty. The individual flaws are hidden in the joining of voice to voice.

What a wonderful day we are living in! This is not the time to be individualistic. It is time to let the river flow. Lift up your voices together, singing in the Spirit, worshiping the King of Glory and letting *"the sound of many waters"* come forth.

In the summer of 1998, I received an e-mail message from Malaysia:

> I attend a Charismatic Methodist church, and the Lord has been doing supernatural

things among us. I hear the sound of awakening in the Spirit realm, the sound of revival coming forth from Malaysia. We are all so excited, and I just don't know how to express myself in words.

The Lord has touched me in many ways while I read the *Glory* book. I didn't go past Chapter 1 for a few days because of the incredible anointing of the Lord. I just couldn't go on except to worship Him and Him alone.

I am new in the area of dreams and visions, but I saw twice the same dream. I was standing before a great door, experiencing gushes of wind hitting my face, as if it was the breath of God. I felt as if I was flying with each gust of wind that hit my face. This added to my spirit a fullness of the love, joy, excitement, peace, goodness, mercy, the fullness of God that is beyond comprehension.

I heard in the distance the sound of worship arising to the heavens as the sound of many waters. I felt myself energized and began to shout excitedly. Words could not describe what I felt in my spirit.

This is just one of the miraculous things that are happening in our prayer group in the Methodist Church in Malaysia.

Isn't that exciting! We are coming together into the flow.

Our independent spirits must flee away, and we must reach out, taking one another by the hand, and move together, as waves of the glory of God wash over us.

Our independent spirits must flee away, and we must reach out, taking one another by the hand, and move together, as waves of the glory of God wash over us. Let us lift up our voices until they become the voice of the Spirit of God calling forth to the people in this last day, as *"the sound of many waters."* May our voices speak forth sounds of glory, and may those sounds become as the voice of God speaking forth to a generation that will come into the fullness of God in this last-day move of His Spirit.

It is wonderful to be able to flow in the river of God, but to be able to flow together in the river is nothing short of a miracle. God knows how to take people from the West and people from the South and people from the East and people from the North and meld us all together into one great flow of His river.

Being able to flowing individually is wonderful, but God wants to bring forth a people who can flow together to the goodness of the Lord. If we can learn to flow together, we can have revival.

God has ordained that we flow together:

> *Then thou shalt see, and FLOW TOGETHER, and thine heart shall fear, and be enlarged; because the abundance of the sea shall be converted unto thee, the forces of the Gentiles shall come unto thee.*   Isaiah 60:5

> *Therefore they shall come and sing in the height of Zion, and shall FLOW TOGETHER to the goodness of the LORD, for wheat, and for wine, and for oil, and for the young of the flock and of the herd: and their soul shall be as a watered garden; and they shall not sorrow any more at all.*   Jeremiah 31:12

In the early summer of 1998, Monsignor Walsh invited me to speak at the Catholic priests' retreat in Malvern, Pennsylvania. About seventy-five priests from the East Coast and other parts of the country gathered. I had been privileged to speak at Catholic lay-leaders' conferences in England and in other parts of the world, but this was my first priests' conference. God poured out His Spirit upon us there in a most glorious fashion.

They had a little different flow than I was accustomed to, so I found myself in a new situation. The
first night of the services, the Monsignor stepped
up and took me by the hand. I had my eyes closed,
and we were praising and worshiping the Lord, but
when he took my hand something wonderful happened. In the uniting of our hands, suddenly the
individual flows were merged into one great flow.
Rather than two separate flows, we now had one.

**In the uniting of our hands, suddenly
the individual flows were merged
into one great flow. Rather than two
separate flows, we now had one.**

One of the priests who was a part of the ministry
team was also a member of the Catholic/Pentecos-
tal Dialogue Committee. His comment the next day
was this: "I wanted to see what is happening between Catholics and Pentecostals, and I take from
here a picture forever embedded in my memory. It
is of the Monsignor (representing the Catholics) and
Ruth (the Pentecostals) as they were joined hand in
hand, dancing, swaying, moving together by the
Spirit of God. I will never forget it."

It happened because each of us was willing to

make an adjustment to our distinct flow for the glory
of God and the benefit of the Body of Christ. We
sometimes have to make such adjustments, but
when it is accomplished and we can flow together,
God honors it. A river made up of the flow of two
people can sweep over others and, in the process,
add to its strength. It can very quickly be multiplied
to twenty and then to two hundred and two thousand. As the water flows, it can be multiplied until
it becomes a vast flow affecting the lives of countless believers. We can and we must learn to flow
together to the goodness of the Lord.

When we begin to realize in the realm of the Spirit
what God is doing in this day and hour and we gain
an ability to flow together, an enlargement will
come. This enlargement that many of us seek cannot come until we learn to flow together.

It is difficult for some to comprehend the greatness of what God is doing. He is lifting the scales
from our eyes, causing walls to fall down and removing the many divisions among us. In another
Catholic conference last summer, every day the
aisles and the altar area were full of people who were
out under the power of God. There was not a single
open spot where another person could lie down.
Priests were out of their seats, going up and down
the aisles and in and out of the pews, laying hands
on the heads of the people. It was a marvelous ex-

perience. We are seeing a sudden acceleration of spiritual activity because we are so near to the coming of the Lord. There is unity in the river of God.

God wants to send forth rivers of living waters from our innermost being, but we must remove the dams. We can no longer allow bitterness, envy, or strife to hinder the flow of the river of God. We cannot afford to allow anything that other people say or do to us to hinder that flow.

I don't know America nearly as well as I do other places because I have been away too long, but I know that in Jerusalem we have hundreds of individualistic people who come to serve the Lord. Most of them have never learned to flow with anybody else. God wants a people that can flow together for His glory. This is not my river, and it is not your river. It is God's river, and it belongs to all His children, the Body of Christ universal. We will have to learn to flow with Baptists, Methodists, Presbyterians, Episcopalians, Catholics, and Orthodox alike. The name is unimportant. Learn to yield to the Holy Spirit and flow together with your diverse brethren.

We will never flow together in our minds. The Living Creatures that Ezekiel saw were not joined together at the head. We will not learn to flow together by sitting down and coming to some common understanding. We will be joined together at the wings, the place of soaring. It is our wings that enable us to soar together in the Spirit, and that is how we will be joined. Our joining will be in the flow of the river of God.

God wants to send forth rivers of living waters from our innermost being, but we must remove the dams. We can no longer allow bitterness, envy or strife to hinder the flow of the river of God. We cannot afford to allow anything that other people say or do to us to hinder that flow. Let the Lord use His dynamite to remove those dams now. Remove the dam called "the opinions of men." Remove the dam called "the fear of men." Remove the dam called "the desire to please men." Let your only desire be to yield to the life-giving waters of God's river.

When people are hungry for God, whether they are Hindus or Buddhists or Muslims or Jewish people or New Agers, God visits them. In Jerusalem God is visiting both the Arabs and the Jews and causing them to have visions and dreams and revelations of who Jesus is. Very soon now we will all know as Peter that God is *no respecter of persons.*

God is reaching out to the Muslim world and

sending great Holy Ghost revival, and if He can do it among the Muslims, why would you doubt that He can do it among the people of your church? Church after church will be swept up in the great flow of His river. Tear down the barriers that have been built up in your own mind.

It is not a time to concern ourselves with minors. Let us stick to the majors. If we get caught up in the struggle over small things, we might miss what God is doing.

Last summer, a Presbyterian brother began to sing a new song in our campmeeting, and God said that whereas in the past the waves of revival that people of various denominations rode seemed to be short, those waves were now lengthening. As we lose sight of each other and get our eyes focused on the Lord of the river, we will be lost in His very presence and lifted up to His very throne. Then He can begin to show us things we have never seen before. He is ready to show us things to come.

It is not a time to concern ourselves with minors. Let us stick to the majors. If we get caught up in the struggle over small things, we might miss what God is doing. Concentrate on the river, on getting into the river and on letting go and being carried away with it. Stop worrying about every little point of doctrinal difference. Let go and flow.

Is it possible that there will be reconciliation between the various divisions in Christianity? Absolutely, and quickly. It is being brought about by the flow of the river. As we all get out into deeper waters, we are being swept along together. We couldn't do it, but God is doing it by His Spirit.

We have boxed ourselves in far too much and placed too many limitations on ourselves. We are very slow to move outside of self-imposed limits of denomination, conference, church, family, neighborhood and locality. God desires a people who can swim comfortably in any part of His river.

When it comes to worshiping with people who are quite different than us, many say, "I just can't worship with people who believe like that." When we get in the realm of the Spirit, we are not having doctrinal discussions. We are touched by the Spirit, and the person next to us is touched by the Spirit. We are being carried out in the flow of it, and they are being carried out in the flow of it. Our heart is moved to praise, and their heart is moved to praise. In the realm of the Spirit, our focus of attention and their focus of attention is the Lord, and doctrine plays a less significant role.

"What doctrine?" When you are lost in the flow

of the river, you can't even remember what a doctrine is. All you know is that you are in the river, and you are swimming, and your love for Jesus is overwhelming. Nothing else matters.

When the river is flowing in us and we are flowing in the river, we will no longer ask each other about denominational background or affiliation. It is not relevant.

Ezekiel saw a great variety of fish being harvested from this river. They will not all be alike. Get ready for variety. Get rid of your hang-ups. Get over any biases you still have. God wants a variety in His family.

When the river is flowing in us and we are flowing in the river, we will no longer ask each other about denominational background or affiliation. It is not relevant. If you are a child of God and I am a child of God, that's all that matters. If we all belong to the King of kings and Lord of lords, what purpose is served by interjecting division? Body of Christ, Bride of Christ, Family of God, Fellow Laborers in Christ, get on with the revival! Let unity come in the flow of the river, in *River Glory*.

Chapter 14

Harvest in the River

And it shall come to pass, that every thing that liveth, which moveth, whithersoever the rivers shall come, shall live: and THERE SHALL BE A VERY GREAT MULTITUDE OF FISH, because these waters shall come thither: for they shall be healed; and every thing shall live whither the river cometh. And it shall come to pass, that the fishers shall stand upon it from Engedi even unto Eneglaim; they shall be a place to spread forth nets; THEIR FISH SHALL BE ACCORDING TO THEIR KINDS, AS THE FISH OF THE GREAT SEA, EXCEEDING MANY.   Ezekiel 47:9-10

"Their fish shall be ... as the fish of the great sea, exceeding many." There is a great harvest in this river, and it is time for the ingathering of the fish.

In the days to come, we will not just harvest individual fish, but entire schools of fish will be taken. Some have yet to realize that there are fish in these waters. How could there not be? These are life-giving waters. Every kind of fish is to be found there: *"exceeding many."*

I don't know if we can comprehend that or not. We would be happy if there were great fish or many fish, but God has promised us *"exceeding many."* This harvest will not be one we can count. It will not be one we can measure. It will not be one we can easily evaluate.

In the days to come, we will not just harvest individual fish, but entire schools of fish will be taken.

Jesus called His disciples to be *"fishers of men."* Some must have wondered what He meant by that. He was from Nazareth, an inland town, and there was no place for fishing there. The disciples, on the other hand, were from traditional fishing families who lived and worked around the Sea of Galilee. They had the best boats and the best fishing businesses in the area, yet here was a man who had never

caught a fish telling them they were going to become fisherman under His leadership.

One day, after Jesus had stood in one of Peter's
boats and taught the people gathered on the shore
of the Sea of Galilee, He turned to Peter and said:

> *Launch out into the deep, and let down your*
> *nets for a draught.* Luke 5:4

These gifted fishermen must have been offended
by this suggestion. They had, Peter said, *"toiled all*
night long," yet they had caught nothing. Would cast-
ing their nets one more time change anything?

Because they respected Jesus, they could not
refuse. Peter said:

> *Master, we have toiled all the night, and have*
> *taken nothing: nevertheless at thy word I will*
> *let down the net.* Luke 5:5

The result amazed everyone:

> *And when they had this done, they enclosed a*
> *great multitude of fishes: and their net brake.*
> Luke 5:6

There were more fish than they could carry, and
they were forced to seek help from another ship. This

is the kind of harvest our Lord delights in supplying, and won't it be wonderful when we can involve all of our brothers and their boats? We won't wait to see what name is on the boat or where its nets were manufactured. We won't be concerned whether the harvest helpers came from a certain Bible school or seminary. We will not be concerned about checking the credentials of the person manning the boat and of those working the nets. There will be such a great harvest of fish that we will be forced to shout, "Help! Somebody! Anybody! Anyone who has a boat! Anyone who has a net! Help me so that the fish will not be lost!"

There will be more than enough fish to fill my church and more than enough for your church. We won't be fighting over who gets which fish. Our only concern will be that the fish are not lost. Our concern will be to get them into the boat, any boat. The greatness of the harvest will take from us the spirit of competition. There is no competitiveness in the river.

When you are accustomed to being in the glory realm, the spirit of competition can no longer satisfy you. You are appalled by it.

In our family, all four of us — my father, my mother, my brother and myself — were preachers, and yet there was no spirit of competition among us. Whoever was preaching was cheered on and amened by the other three preachers in the family.

When we get in the glory and begin to harvest, all thought of competition is gone. We no longer care if people have perfect voices. We no longer care if ours are the best trained people around. We don't have time to check and see if every detail is perfectly in order. When revival comes, God takes charge.

He is working in us, changing us, making us want only to be part of the end-time harvest, nothing more. If we are part of what God is doing in the Earth, we won't worry about who gets the credit for everything.

> In every way possible, God is letting us know that the harvest we will see in this last day will surpass the measurements we have grown accustomed to using.

It is time to get the harvest uppermost in our minds. If I see you throw out your nets, may I always be willing to lend my strength to help you bring them in. This revival will be bigger than all of us, and most churches will not have enough room to contain the catch that will come to them.

When Jesus preached to the multitudes, there were five thousand men present, not counting the women

and the children. Another time when He preached
to a great crowd, they counted four thousand men,
and again they didn't even count the women and
children. That all happened in a very small country
with a very small population. When the Lord speaks
about a multitude, therefore, He is speaking of some
very big numbers. The harvest we can expect, however, will be more than just a multitude. It will be *a
very great multitude.*" If that was not clear enough,
He went on to refer to the fish as *"exceeding many."*
In every way possible, God is letting us know that
the harvest we will see in this last day will surpass
the measurements we have grown accustomed to
using.

When the disciples caught their great *"draught of
fishes,"* there was something they had to do. They
had to launch out into the deep and cast their nets.
This time, however, we have a very different picture: *"there shall be a very great multitude of fish, because
these waters shall come thither."* The only reason for
this harvest will be the river itself. No man can take
credit for this stirring. No man can glory in this
catch. The harvest is a result of the flowing of the
great river, and no man will be able to deny that
fact.

This harvest will not be a struggle. This harvest
will not be reaped by the sweat of our brow. Fish

will be harvested because of the waters of the river and for no other reason.

This harvest will not be a struggle. This harvest will not be reaped by the sweat of our brow. Fish will be harvested because of the waters of the river and for no other reason.

The area mentioned in the prophecy of Ezekiel, *"from Engedi even unto Eneglaim,"* would cover a very large territory. Imagine all those square miles of spread nets. Every restraint will be removed from our churches, and we will be free to spread our nets. God will remove all the obstacles and make room for us. We don't need elaborate and costly buildings in which to meet. We just need more space to lay out the nets. Use the bulk of the funds for harvesting, not for making the flock more comfortable.

Cleaning fish does not require all the latest technology. Put more of your money into preparing nets and boats to launch so that the harvest can be taken.

When my parents were still young, they pastored a small church in Quantico, Virginia, a marine town. When Orson Wells' famous radio program, "The War of the Worlds" (the portrayal of an unexpected attack from outer space), came on the air, it shocked people all over America and caused many to turn to God. My parents remembered tough marines kneeling and praying in the streets of Quantico. We will soon see a similar thing happening all around us.

You may think that you have been bold for God, but what we are about to see will change us all. Each of us will lose any inhibitions we still have. We will forget about our pride as we see a vast number of people hungering for God.

Many of us have been burdened by the fact that the religious liberties of our children have been reduced in their schools. We need not worry. In the near future, school buildings will be thrown open wide for revival meetings. Those who have most opposed prayer in our schools will themselves be praying in public places. What an exciting day to be living!

If God has stirred you and me and the person next to us, let us believe that He will stir others also and send revival into their hearts. Let the river flow, for wherever it flows, a great harvest is assured.

Some of you might be saying, "But I am not fully prepared for such a harvest." Don't worry. God would rather train His own. He is tired of the world training His people. He can give us on-the-job training. If you will listen to the voice of God and will make a concerted effort in the next few months to tidy up your affairs, you will find yourself in the midst of the ripened harvest field with a sickle in your hand. Because of our advanced technology, perhaps it would be better to say that you will be driving a great spiritual harvest combine. Whatever the case, you can have a part in the great last-day harvest of the Earth. It's in the river, in *River Glory*.

Chapter 15

Healing in the River

And he showed me a pure river of water of life, clear as crystal, proceeding out of the throne of God and of the Lamb. In the midst of the street of it, and on either side of the river, was there the tree of life, which bare twelve manner of fruits, and yielded her fruit every month: and THE LEAVES OF THE TREE WERE FOR THE HEALING OF THE NATIONS.

Revelation 22:1-2

"The leaves of the tree were for the healing of the nations." There is healing in the river, and we are experiencing greater and greater physical miracles as we step deeper into its waters.

When we become conscious that a miracle flow is present, we can just jump into the river and receive the miracle of healing we need.

When we become conscious that a
miracle flow is present, we can just
jump into the river and receive the
miracle of healing we need.

Last summer we experienced many miracles of
healing during our campmeeting. One lady came
with a group from the Wellsley Park Assembly of
God in Whelan, Massachusetts. She had undergone
serious back surgery four months earlier and would
not normally have been out and about yet. Her spine
had been fused and she had three pieces of steel in-
serted in her back. She brought plenty of pain
medicine with her and was sure she would be
spending most of her time in bed. Although it had
been a long car ride to get to the camp, she was so
hungry for God that she came into the first service
that night. When I prayed for her, she began feeling
a change in her body and started walking on her
own without using her cane. She was sure she
wouldn't be able to sleep that night, but she slept
"like a baby."

The next morning she went to the eleven o'clock
service and was prayed for again. She wasn't sure if
God had melted the steel or what He had done, but

she was so free that she was jumping in the presence of God. She was ecstatic.

Another sister came who had undergone a lot of reconstructive surgery done on her leg. I saw her getting her miracle that night as the river was flowing. We had been believing, and we had been worshiping, and every night we had been getting a little deeper into the river.

In the flow of the river there are miracles for your body, for your ministry, for your finances. There are miracles for your children You don't have to make it happen. Just get into the flow and the miracles will be there. This river transforms. Its life-giving waters will loose you from the past and bring you into revival.

Every night great things were done as people were on the floor under the power of God. Many had wonderful visions. Others were having other great experiences in God. Many were healed. This is the day of the river flowing, and there is healing in its waters. Let it flow through you.

As I was coming into the service one night, I met a man from Texas. He said he was not able to stay for the service and requested prayer. He had come to our area for surgery on a herniated disk in his neck, but he had heard of the miracles God was doing at the campmeeting.

"Are you in pain now?" I asked.

"Oh, I'm in excruciating pain!" he answered.

I laid my hand on his head and prayed, and instantly all the pain left.

Another night when God gave me a word that He was healing migraine headaches, a lady told me that she got them frequently and that when she did, it usually took several days to get over them. God healed her instantly.

In the flow of the river there are miracles for your body, for your ministry, for your finances. There are miracles for your children You don't have to make it happen. Just get into the flow and the miracles will be there.

It reminded me of the time, many years before, when we had prayed for a young Methodist boy in my father's tent meeting in Fredericksburg, Virginia. He was to be operated on the next day for cancer of the ear. I looked at his ear, expecting to see an open sore, but there was none. The earlobe was a little blue, but nothing else seemed to be different on that ear.

My father put his hand under the boy's earlobe, I placed my hand on his head, and we began to pray. While we were praying, my father felt something drop into his hand. He looked down, and there were two growths, one about the size of a bean and the other about the size of a pea. They had dropped out of that ear and into his hand.

I looked closely to see if I could detect some opening through which the cancers had dropped, but I could not detect any.

My father held the growths in his hand for a while and let everyone in the meeting see them so that they could rejoice and praise God. Then he put them into a Kleenex and threw them away.

The young man went to the hospital the next day for the operation, and his doctor tested him and declared that he had nothing wrong with his ear and did not need the scheduled operation. He had been totally healed by the power of God.

Somebody later said, "Why didn't you have that matter tested?"

My father's answer was, "With people that believe, they believe whether something is tested or not, and those who don't believe won't believe even if it is tested." If you need to test these things, do, but God desires to have a people that just trust Him and believe Him.

We will see greater and greater things as the days

progress. As we have seen, in this river there is a
flow of healing capable of touching every nation of
the Earth, and no nation will remain untouched by
it in the days ahead. As the flow of the Spirit of God
spreads out to every nation, it will bring healing in
every sense of the word: for body, soul and spirit.

> We will see greater and greater
> things as the days progress. In this
> river there is a flow of healing ca-
> pable of touching every nation of the
> Earth, and no nation will remain un-
> touched by it in the days ahead.

Recently, I was speaking on a telecast in Houston
about the river and its healing power. God gave me
a word of knowledge for someone who was suffer-
ing in the head, chest and lungs. He said He was
healing them right then.

Two nights later a sister who was leading the
praise and worship in the service took time to tes-
tify. She had undergone surgery for cancer the week
before and was home recovering from the operation
when she was impressed to turn on her television
and tune in the program just as I was calling out the
word of knowledge for her. As I declared healing,

all her pain, which had been intense, left her body. It was a great miracle that she was back leading the worship two nights later.

We have had many cases of people's eyes being healed recently. Two people who had been declared "legally blind" were healed in one recent meeting.

What wonderful days! Get into the flow of God's river and experience His healing for yourself.

In one of my meetings with the Catholics last summer a man came who could not kneel. God gave him a great miracle. Suddenly he was touched by the power of God and knelt for more than half an hour without assistance from anyone and without anything to lean against. He was completely healed by the power of God. When the river is flowing, it happens so easily.

Some years ago my brother was praying for a man who had no eardrum. He was saying, "Lord, create an eardrum for him so that he can hear."

Our God is a God of miracles, a God of the unusual, a God of the impossible. Don't try to tell Him how to do it. The river is here and there is healing in its life-giving flow, the flow of River Glory.

The Lord answered him and said, "I don't have to create an eardrum for him to hear. I can make him hear without an eardrum."

When that understanding came to my brother, God instantly gave the man his miracle. He could hear perfectly — without an eardrum. Our God is a God of miracles, a God of the unusual, a God of the impossible. Don't try to tell Him how to do it. The river is here and there is healing in its life-giving flow, the flow of *River Glory*.

Chapter 16

Signs and Wonders and Exploits in the River

Behold, I and the children whom the LORD hath given me are FOR SIGNS AND FOR WONDERS in Israel from the LORD of hosts, which dwelleth in mount Zion. Isaiah 8:18

"For signs and for wonders ..." Amazing signs and wonders await us in the river of God.

This present revival will be marked by the miraculous, by signs and wonders. It will not happen because of our state-of-the-art equipment but because the Miracle Worker is present and is allowed to work. It will happen because of the expectation of our spirits and because we let the river flow.

God has promised to show forth *"signs and wonders"* in these last days, but I am more and more convinced that *we* are the signs and wonders. We will not just experience signs and wonders; we will become signs and wonders to the world. Believe for it and move into it, for it is happening all around us.

As we move forward into revival, we can also expect many and varied signs from Heaven. During our winter campmeeting in 1998 we began to experience something new. Gold dust began to appear on people's faces and hands and clothing. At first it did not happen in the fullness we might have desired, but when God does something and we appreciate it, He does more.

As we move forward into revival, we can also expect many and varied signs from Heaven.

Sister Jane Lowder had come back from South America at Christmas time and was telling us about a lady named Silvana who had gold dust appearing on her while she was worshiping the Lord. Jane brought a video to show us what was happening. During a service, while the sister was worshiping, her face would suddenly be covered with visible flecks of golden dust. The first time Jane saw it she didn't know quite what she was seeing. She wondered why Silvana had put glitter all over her face. That didn't seem to be necessary. Was this some new cosmetic craze? She had prayed for Silvana about a

year before, and she was baptized in the Holy Ghost.
What was happening with her now?

As Sister Jane began to inquire, she discovered that
the golden dust was something that God was giving the sister supernaturally. It seemed to flow from
her scalp. On occasion, her Brazilian pastor would
open his Bible and she would shake the gold dust
from her head onto the Bible. Little piles of gold dust
would fall into the open Bible. The pastor, recog-
nizing how miraculous this was, took that golden
dust and anointed the people with it, and great
miracles were reported among them as a result.

We rejoiced when we saw the video, but we had
no idea that soon God would be manifesting gold
dust in our meetings in Ashland. It happened within
a few weeks of viewing the video. During our winter campmeeting it happened ten or twelve times in
our services.

One morning, during our Spring '98 Ladies' Con-
vention, we showed the video from Brazil of the gold
dust. After the service, one of the ladies went into
the rest room and changed her clothes for the drive
home. She heard something fall to the floor and
thought it must be the brooch she had been wear-
ing. She stooped to pick it up, but to her amazement,
what she picked up was a gold nugget. Needless to
say, she didn't go home that day. She brought it back
into the meeting so that everyone could see what
God had done and rejoice. When God sends some-

thing supernatural into our midst, He deserves all the glory.

A group of six very dignified ladies came to that conference from New Orleans. They were skeptical, not only of the appearance of the gold dust, but also of the laughter that was breaking out in some of the meetings. Their flight was routed through Detroit and, because the plane they were on had some engine trouble, they were delayed there for many hours. Some of the group stayed on the plane, and the others went into the terminal. The ladies who went into the terminal began to notice that gold dust was appearing on them while they were waiting for the plane to be repaired, and after they got back on the plane, laughter broke out with several members of the group. Because they had been skeptical of these experiences, God had to give them these manifestations in a most unlikely place — the Detroit airport.

In August Silvana came from Brazil to visit us. There was such a presence of God with her that I instantly began to cry when I met her. Our people witnessed the miracle taking place in her, and others experienced it as they worshiped. God brought a new dimension of the miraculous into our lives, and before the summer was over, this phenomena was appearing more and more among us. Nearly every time I preached gold dust appeared on my face and on the people who were attending.

In September, after campmeeting was over, I went to Jerusalem. Gold dust appeared in our services there with Nancy Bergen. I also spoke for the Messianic congregation that meets at Christ Church inside Jaffa Gate, and it happened there as well.

Recently I ministered at the Friendship Baptist Church in Atlanta, Georgia. In the first service Pastor Bob Shattles had oil appear in his hands. There must have been a quarter of a cup of it. He was carried away in the Spirit to Heaven and experienced the throne of God. The next morning in the service his hands were again flowing with oil and that night as he was speaking I saw gold dust on his face. When I mentioned it to him later, he said, "I know. I felt it happen."

The following Sunday morning (I was not there, but he told me by phone) gold dust came down from Heaven in their morning service and all his people saw it happen. That night, as they were getting ready to go back to the evening service, several of his members saw gold dust falling from their hair as they combed it. It had evidently been there from the morning service.

I have noticed that the gold dust we are experiencing in our meetings sometimes comes through the pores of the skin on the face or hands or some other part of the body of those who are worshiping the Lord, and sometimes it flows down from Heaven, falling on either the people or their clothing or on something inside the church building. Recently, however, I have watched it as it was being created before my very eyes.

Not long ago I was on a television program called Pinnacle on Channel 55 in Orlando, Florida, being interviewed by Brother Claude Bowers. It had been a wonderful half hour, but just as we were about to go off the air, I looked across at Brother Bower and saw a flake of gold dust under his left eye. Before I realized it, I had said before the entire television audience to hear, "Brother Bowers, you have gold dust on your face, under your left eye." It took only that one flake of gold dust to bring a large crowd of people from Central Florida to our opening meeting in Mt. Dora, a town of some eight thousand residents. That's what signs are all about.

> *And by the hands of the apostles were many signs and wonders wrought among the people ... and believers were the more added to the Lord, multitudes both of men and women.*
>
> Acts 5:12-14

Don't be afraid of what will happen to you and how you will react to it when you get into God's river, and when unusual things begin to happen, don't be too quick to judge. I have observed that when we see something unusual happen suddenly to others, we doubt its authenticity. When it happens to us, however, we are immediately sure it is of God.

I have observed that when we see something unusual happen suddenly to others, we doubt its authenticity. When it happens to us, however, we are immediately sure it is of God.

One pastor in India complained that I was teaching the women of the conference how to dance. I was encouraging them to yield themselves to the Lord, but I certainly wasn't teaching them how to dance. He went around one day causing quite a disturbance, getting all the pastors upset about this matter. The next day, however, the power of God hit him in one of the meetings, and he began to dance.

In South India, the men wear *dhotis*, which are nothing more than a piece of cloth wrapped around the lower part of their bodies. There are no pins or belts or snaps or buttons to hold the *dhoti* up. It is held up by a simple fold of the cloth at the waist. This pastor proceeded to dance so wildly, knocking over chairs and twirling from one end of the room to the other, that his *dhoti* began to come loose and was threatening to fall off. Finally, he came to himself, grabbed hold of his *dhoti* and said, "That was God." When it happened to him, it took him just a moment to realize that it was real.

When gold dust began appearing on us in the campmeeting services, it was not because we had ever asked the Lord for gold dust. We didn't know what to ask for. We just said, "Lord we are willing to be signs and wonders in this last-day move of the Spirit. Whatever it is that You want to do and however You want to do it, we are willing." The appearance of the gold dust was one of the results of that prayer.

Many times, when laughter was first appearing in the church, I heard people laughing and thought to myself that it was probably because they had been to some laughing revival meeting. When I checked out this theory, however, I found that many of those who were laughing had never been in a Pentecostal meeting of any kind. Laughter was just their response to coming into contact with the powerful life-giving waters of the river.

I was invited to speak to a group of people in the southern tip of New Zealand. The meetings were scheduled for the fellowship hall of a Presbyterian church, but such a large crowd gathered that the pastor opened the church and moved the crowd inside. It was a very classical Presbyterian church, a little more ornate than most of those we know here in

America, and the crowd was so large that it filled
the platform and even the high altar. Toward the
end of the service, a lady fell on the high altar and
began to laugh. I was blessed by her laughing, but I
assumed that she had been to one of the laughing
revivals. I was told later that she was a visitor from
the northern part of New Zealand and had never
been in that type of meeting before. That night she
was saved, filled with the Holy Ghost and had the
revelation of revival. Although she had never seen
anyone laugh uncontrollably in church, this was her
uninhibited response to the Holy Ghost.

> **These experiences have taught me
> not to make judgments about where
> people are in their Christian experi-
> ence. God is bringing people into new
> realms.**

These experiences have taught me not to make
judgments about where people are in their Christian experience. God is bringing people into new
realms. In a few moment's time, He is doing things
in their lives that they never thought they would
experience. I have seen people so overwhelmed with
joy that they worked both legs and both arms at
once, almost like a child having a temper tantrum,

except that this was good. Who am I to question what God does in the river?

Get ready for new and exciting experiences. This river is taking us in new directions, and when we decide to flow with it, we become more full of God than ever before. In the future, we will be so full of God that people will look at us and declare, "They are in the river, and the river is in them." What a glorious day!

When we are caught away in the river, we are taken out of the realm of our own reasoning and brought into God's realm, where we become totally dependent upon Him.

When we are caught away in the river, we are taken out of the realm of our own reasoning and brought into God's realm, where we become totally dependent upon Him. Jump in without fear.

If God wants to cover you in gold dust, let Him do it. If He wants to make you a wonder and a sign, let Him do it. Worship the King and let His supernatural replace your natural. Let Him carry you out into the depths. Let Him take you from glory to glory.

Because we have been afraid of the unknown, we have only begun to see what God can do for us. He desires to carry us out so quickly into the depths that we will look at one another in amazement.

If we allow the river to flow through us, all those around us will be blessed. Not one will remain untouched by it. When God's river flows, there is an accompanying revelation of His glory and demonstration of His power. God is revealed in the midst of us through miracles and signs and wonders. Don't hinder it; let it happen.

During our summer campmeeting I saw in the Spirit what I can only describe as "glory balls" on the feet of the people. Their feet seemed to be surrounded by the glory of God. I sensed that this would bring them into a new liberty in dancing and that their dancing would represent a possessing of nations and kingdoms. Let your feet be released in the glory realm. Let the river flow. If you will get into the flow of God's river, you can expect great signs and wonders to happen in your meetings too.

While attending a Randy Clark conference in Oklahoma City I laid hands on a group of ministers who had been invited to the Upper Room at the great Metro Church. Someone asked me to tell about the signs and wonders God is showing forth in this revival and, after hearing about these great things, a group of the ministers lined up for prayer. As I prayed for them, they began falling out under the power of God. One pastor faxed me later to say that it was the first time he had ever been slain in the spirit. When he got up, he said, his lips were covered with gold dust.

Because we have been afraid of the unknown, we have only begun to see what God can do for us. He desires to carry us out so quickly into the depths that we will look at one another in amazement.

Another brother sent a fax. He had been healed in our meeting in Phoenix, Arizona. He fell out under the power several times in the service that night. When he got home and was undressing, he discovered gold dust on the inside of his shirt. He hadn't realized at the time what God was doing for him and only saw it later.

That morning we heard the same news from three different cities. God's Spirit is not being poured out in isolated cases. He is doing it everywhere people are hungry.

In November of 1997, during one of our weekend revival meetings in Ashland, I stepped up to the pulpit to preach one night and was suddenly carried away in the Spirit. I could feel myself being rapidly lifted upward. I must have been carried away for at least a half hour to forty-five minutes and during that time everything in the meeting just stopped.

When I came to myself there was a rhythm that was repeating itself over and over in my spirit. Very slowly I heard myself saying, "The eyes of the blind shall see; the ears of the deaf shall hear; and the dead shall be raised to life again." Again, "The eyes of the blind shall see; the ears of the deaf shall hear; and the dead shall be raised to life again."

The people had been sitting all this time in the glory, and some later said that it was the greatest glory they had ever experienced. Still, it was a strange experience. One would naturally think that if the Lord had wanted to carry me away, why had He not done it while I was sitting on the platform earlier in the service? The fact that He had waited until I was at the pulpit showed me that He obviously wanted everything to come to a stop and for that great glory to come in.

There were other things that the Lord showed me that night, but less than a week later we took several carloads of our camp people to the funeral of a pastor in Fredericksburg, Virginia. Just before the funeral service started, my associate, Ruth Carneal, who was seated next to me on the front row, turned to me and asked where the rest room was. I pointed it out at the back of the church.

"Would I have time to go before the service begins?" she asked.

"Please do," I answered her.

When she didn't return I assumed that she had taken a seat farther back in the sanctuary.

I'm not sure how much time elapsed. I had a part in the ceremony and several other pastors read scripture portions. After a time, however (probably fifteen or twenty minutes), someone tapped me on the shoulder and said, "Sister Ruth Carneal is on the floor at the back." I got up and went back quietly, not wanting to disturb the service. When I saw Ruth stretched out on the floor, I knew immediately that she was dead.

My first thought was not to spoil the funeral, so I got two brothers to pick her up, one by the feet and the other by the shoulders, and to carry her into a side room. It was a small room, and there wasn't enough space to stretch her body out completely, so the men sat her up on a chair. Her head was falling to one side, so I reached over to support her head and neck.

Until that moment, my only concern had been to get her away from the funeral service so that it would not be disturbed. As I placed my hand on Ruth's neck, suddenly those rhythms from the week before returned to my spirit. The words came to me just as slowly and distinctly and powerfully as they had that night: "The eyes of the blind shall see; the ears of the deaf shall hear; and the dead shall be raised to life again." I was not saying the words out loud; they were going over and over in my spirit. "The eyes of the blind shall see; the ears of the deaf shall hear; and the dead shall be raised to life again." When I said it the second time within myself, she gasped and her spirit came back into her.

Someone had called an ambulance and by this time it had arrived. The paramedics quickly placed Ruth into the ambulance and headed for the hospital. I was able to ride in the front seat of the ambulance with them. In the rear they were doing a preliminary examination of Ruth and they found that all her vital signs were normal. When we arrived at the Emergency Room and doctors had thoroughly examined Ruth, they discovered that when she had gone to the rest room she had suffered a severe hemorrhage and lost fully a third of her blood. This had caused her to faint and die as she came out of the rest room.

It had been an awesome experience when I was first carried away and again that day when the rhythms of the river came to me, but the most amazing thing about this experience came to me later. I had never actually prayed for her to come back to life. The miracle happened in the flow of the river.

Recently, Ruth was in a meeting in the Royal The-
atre in New Castle in Australia. In the morning
service, everyone present heard the audible voice
of the Lord coming through the public address sys-
tem. He was saying, "This will be a revival of signs.
Thank me." They all sat in amazement, seeing that
no one was speaking into the microphones and re-
alizing that they had heard the audible voice of the
Lord. In describing His voice, they said it "had fire
on it."

**Nothing will be impossible to us in
the days ahead as we move further
into *River Glory*.**

Did not John the Revelator report?

> *I was in the Spirit on the Lord's day, and heard
> behind me a great voice, as of a trumpet.*
>   Revelation 1:10

Get it into your spirit today: "The eyes of the blind
shall see; the ears of the deaf shall hear; and the dead
shall be raised to life again." Nothing will be impossible to us in the days ahead as we move further
into *River Glory*.

Chapter 17

Joy and Security in the River

God is our refuge and strength, a very present help in trouble. Therefore will not we fear, though the earth be removed, and though the mountains be carried into the midst of the sea; Though the waters thereof roar and be troubled, though the mountains shake with the swelling thereof. Selah. THERE IS A RIVER, the streams whereof shall make glad the city of God, the holy place of the tabernacles of the most High. God is in the midst of her; she shall not be moved: God shall help her, and that right early. Psalm 46:1-5

"There is a river." There is a wonderful sense of security and an accompanying joy that come to us in the flow of the river.

The very existence of the river makes us secure. It

is wonderful just to know that *"there is a river."* We don't have to say, "I think ..." We don't have to surmise. We don't have to wonder. We don't have to ponder. We don't have to question. We know. This river is sure. *"There is a river."*

How could we as people of the river possibly be concerned about the waters of adversity that are coming our way? We know that *"there is a river,"* and that is enough.

In verse 3, the psalmist spoke of other waters, waters that roared, waters that were troubled, waters that were difficult. The Lord is showing us that we will face difficulties in the days ahead. The answer of the Lord, however, is, *"there is a river [and] the streams [of it] make [us] glad."* There is no need for us to be worried, no need for us to be fretful or concerned. When God calls our attention to troubles, He does so because He knows we are river people. He knows that those other waters will not overflow us, distress us, nor disturb us. How could we as people of the river possibly be concerned about the waters of adversity that are coming our way? We know that *"there is a river,"* and that is enough.

We have a sure river, and that river only knows gladness, a gladness that will affect the whole city of God. This river provides security in the time of difficulty, not just for an individual, but for all the people of God. Wherever the people of God are found throughout the whole world, they will be positively affected by these streams of gladness.

The people of the world cannot understand why we are so full of joy. Most of those who are not yet in the river see nothing for which to rejoice, but this joy we feel is supernatural and it emanates from the river.

If we look too long at life's circumstances we may also begin to wonder why we're so happy. There is no way to deny that our joy and sense of security is supernatural. Just because there are troubles all around us is no reason to give in to the world's response to trouble. We are different because we are in the river.

Some Christians have come to the conclusion that they must give in to the world's response so that people around them will feel that they are really in need and pray for them. This is not necessary. God's people must be different. If we are in the river and the river is in us, the flow of its streams will make us glad when no one else is glad.

People should not be able to look at your countenance and know that you have ever had a day of trouble. They should not be able to look at you and know that anyone in your family has ever been difficult. They should not be able to look at you and know that your brothers or sisters sold you into Egypt, or that they plotted something bad against you. People should not be able to detect the smell of smoke on you or to know that you were ever in a fiery furnace.

God is looking for a people who will not be embarrassed with victory. His people have no need to look as if they need a handout. They don't need to have the appearance of those who have suffered many afflictions.

Some people were delivered from the fiery furnace fifty years ago, but you can still smell smoke on them. It seems that those furnaces still belch out their smoke periodically. If the smoke is not there, these people somehow will it to come. They glory in it. How sad!

God is looking for a people who will not be embarrassed with victory. His people have no need to look as if they need a handout. They don't need to have the appearance of those who have suffered many afflictions. God's people know the blessing of the river, the victory of the river, the triumph of the river. We refuse to live in stagnant waters. This river suits us fine because it is continually flowing. Its waters are always fresh and clear. They make us glad.

The flow of gladness in and the flow of gladness out, the flow of joy in and the flow of joy out, comes by us, but it doesn't start with us, and we can't keep it for ourselves. This flow is from the river. We can leave a service feeling lighter than when we came in, feeling less tired than when we came in, feeling more strength than when we came in because we have stepped into the river. We can know victory because we have been reminded by the Spirit of God that *"there is a river."* This miracle is not of us. It is because of the river and the security the river brings to our lives.

This psalm was written by the sons of Korah. They were known for their prophecy in song. I can just picture these young men under the anointing of the Holy Ghost singing, *"there is a river."* They were centuries ahead of their time. John the Revelator, hundreds of years later, got the same revelation and said, *"I saw a pure river of water of life."* The sons of Korah were among the first to see it.

The river of God is only known by revelation. Every great river spoken of in the Scriptures was known in this way. These were not rivers that you could put your finger into in the natural. The river of Ezekiel 47 did not exist in the territory the prophet was familiar with. The rivers John saw flowing out of the *"belly"* of believers were revealed rivers. The river of Revelation 21 and 22, that pure river of crystal, was seen only by revelation. This river of God must be glimpsed by revelation and laid hold of by faith. Let us journey to it, pitch our tent beside it and jump in. As we see it from afar, let us reach out and embrace it, and it will become ours.

This river of God must be glimpsed by revelation and laid hold of by faith. Let us journey to it, pitch our tent beside it and jump in.

The sons of Korah saw this river in Jerusalem, and that is notable for Jerusalem is a city without a river. They could see that in the future Jerusalem would have a river because what God does in the supernatural realm He ultimately brings to pass in the natural. It is never done in the reverse order. What we see in the Spirit He brings into the natural. He never copies the natural.

In the future there will be a river flowing out of

Jerusalem. It will flow out and heal the marshy, salty places outside of the city of Jerusalem and go on down into the desert areas. It will bring healing everywhere it flows. The sons of Korah saw it and were able to declare it.

That river, they also were shown in revelation, brings security and joy in the midst of trouble. It doesn't matter if the person you live with has no joy. You can still have a fountain of it inside of you. There may not be a speck of peace in those around you, but you can still have a fountain of peace rising up within you. Those around you may not have any of these things operative in their lives. There is a lot of turmoil in the world around us right now. Still, you can have a security the world only dreams of as you stay in the river.

There is only one reason that we are joyful. It is because *"there is a river"* and because that river brings gladness.

Many people are against the laughter that is coming forth in the revival, but what better sign could there be that the streams that make glad are flowing by? These streams bring gladness, and if you can yield to that gladness and be touched by that gladness, you cannot help but rejoice in the Lord. Supernatural joy will come forth out of the innermost part of your being, and just about the time you think you might cry, you will feel a joy begin to bubble up from within. It just might bubble up so uncontrollably that you, too, begin to laugh.

What else did the psalmists see? *"There is a river, the streams thereof make glad the city of our God, the holy place of the tabernacle of the most high God. God is in the midst of her."* They saw that God was in the midst of the river. No wonder it brings us joy. No wonder it makes us totally secure. God is in the river.

Not only is God in the midst of the river, but He is the river. He is the flow because it is a flow of His Spirit. He is the stream that flows into our lives and out of our lives and which blesses us on the way through.

Joy brings strength. The prophet Nehemiah declared:

> *For this day is holy unto our Lord: neither be ye sorry; for the joy of the LORD is your strength.*
> Nehemiah 8:10

We don't have to stay in the valleys of life. For many years now, we have been hearing preachers speak about the need for us to "go through some valleys," and there is an element of truth in what they say. We can go through a valley, however, without having to shed tears there. We can cross our valleys without becoming sad.

We don't have to live in the valley forever. While

it is true that you must pass through a valley in order to get to the next mountain, I discovered when I was younger and was climbing the mountains of Nepal that some of those valleys are quite elevated. Kathmandu Valley, for instance, lies at about four thousand feet above sea level. After you climb the next mountain, you come to another valley, and that valley lies at six thousand feet above sea level. From there you climb the next mountain, and you find yet another valley, this one at eight thousand feet above sea level. Each new valley is as high, or nearly so, as the mountain leading to it. Up nearer to Mt. Everest some valleys lie at twenty thousand feet above sea level or more. So valleys are not always low places. They are just approaches to the high places.

> If you have to go through some valleys to get to the next high place, don't worry about it. You are still higher than you were before. You are still moving forward.

If you have to go through some valleys to get to the next high place, don't worry about it. You are still higher than you were before, and you are still moving forward.

If you have to come down a little to cross over to the next high place, just keep your sights on the mountain. You don't have to stay in the valley. It is a temporary place for you, and as you cross it, be aware that the river of God is with you.

The city of Jerusalem sits at about two thousand feet above sea level, so the valleys there are already at least that high. When you are in those valleys, you are a lot higher than you were, for instance, at the Dead Sea (which is situated at one thousand, three hundred feet below sea level). You are nearly three thousand, five hundred feet higher than you were when you started, so don't mind the valleys of life. It's all in the way you look at it.

We have feared the valleys and when we had to go through them, our chin was about as low as the valley floor itself. Look up! *"There is a river"* and that river *"makes glad the city of God."*

I made up my mind a number of years ago that I would not be sad or sorrowful again. You might ask, "Can you just make up your mind not to be sad?" Yes, you just take authority over sadness. When the enemy comes and begins to push your buttons to make you sad, you say to him, "Just stay over there. Don't come any nearer."

I refuse to give myself to sadness. I have a great river flowing through me, and this river keeps me happy, no matter what's in my pocket or whether there are people around or whether I am totally alone. No matter what the circumstances of life may be, our happiness is not dependent upon what's happening round about us. It doesn't depend on whether or not we get our favorite thing for Christmas. This joy is supernatural. No matter what America faces in the coming years, the people of the river will not be disturbed by it.

If we live in the river and the river lives in us, we can have a wonderful security in the midst of turmoil.

Here in America, we celebrate Thanksgiving Day. Every year our president must make a resolution that a certain day be set aside to give thanks to God. The purpose of our Thanksgiving is not just to thank God that He brought the early settlers through the winters and gave them a harvest, but we do it because this year God is bringing us through every trial and He is giving us a harvest. There is security in the river because God is there, and His presence brings us supernatural joy. It's to be found in *River Glory.*

Chapter 18

All That You Need in the River

But MY GOD SHALL SUPPLY ALL YOUR NEED according to his riches IN GLORY by Christ Jesus. Philippians 4:19

"My God shall supply all your need ... in glory." There are so many other things we could mention that are to be found in the river. There is, in fact, an abundant supply of anything you can name, all that you will ever need.

There is holiness to be found in the river. Many of us worry about approaching God's throne, thinking that our hearts are not pure enough. It is the river that's pure, not you. You can't be pure unless you are submerged in the purity of the river. When you get into the river, and get *River Glory* into your soul, it happens automatically. Holiness comes from God, not from you. He is holy. Get submerged in the flow of His river, and you will become more like Him.

This river is conducive to repentance. When you feel the great waters of God wash over you, repenting is no longer a struggle. It comes easily. When you do repent, you find a wealth of grace and mercy awaiting you in the river. It is a healing balm which awaits all those who seek God's waters.

Purity of heart is a wonderful thing. Once someone asked my brother, "How do you know when somebody has an evil spirit?"

In the river there is an abundant supply of anything you can name, all that you will ever need.

His inspired reply was: "Have a good spirit yourself." When your spirit is clear, when you are among *"the pure in heart,"* it is not difficult to discern when someone else is not. You discern without trying. There is a clear distinction between the pure and the impure. Get into the pure river of God, and you won't even have to turn on your discerner button. The Spirit of God within you will make you know what is not of Him.

There is great liberty to be found in the river. Many

of us have been familiar with the Holy Spirit and His work for some time now. We have sometimes considered ourselves to be experts, and that has been part of our problem. By thinking we knew exactly how to do it, we have often gotten in the Spirit's way, becoming a hindrance and quenching the Spirit in the process.

Paul instructed the Thessalonian believers:

> *Quench not the Spirit.*
> 1 Thessalonians 5:19

In many circles, when anyone begins to speak in tongues, the worship leader has been instructed to start singing a chorus to drown out the sound so that no one else is "disturbed" by it. When someone begins to dance in the Spirit, ushers have been instructed to sit them down so that they don't draw attention to themselves. We have known everything that we did not want to happen, but too often we have not known what we should want to happen or should expect to happen. We have not learned what the Spirit desires of us, what He wants to do in our midst.

The answer is simple. He is the river. He wants us to present ourselves before Him, an empty channel through which He can flow. He is the river; let Him flow. Give Him room to move. He is the water of life and is looking for a dry river bed that He can inhabit and flow through.

You can never contain this river, and you can never control it. You can only present yourself as a willing channel for its flow. You be the river bed. Let the river of life flow through you, and your bed will become greatly enlarged.

How often we attempt to control the flow of the river for fear that others are just not ready for it! How many times we have hindered the flow of the Spirit because some important person came into the meeting, someone whom we thought was too immature to appreciate spiritual things! *Surely another time would be better for them*, we imagine. We are often wrong.

You can never contain this river, and you can never control it. You can only present yourself as a willing channel for its flow. You be the river bed. Let the river of life flow through you, and your bed will become greatly enlarged.

People have told me many times in Jerusalem, "We have somebody we want to bring to your place, but we want to take them around to a few other places in town first because they're not quite ready for the liberty you enjoy." By the time they take these people around to other places, they are really not ready for what God wants to do. I would rather direct people into the flow of the Spirit and let God do things His way. I have seen people who were totally new to the Gospel be born again, filled with the Holy Ghost and begin to dance before the Lord in a single service. Many open their mouths and begin to prophesy or tell a vision they are having as they are carried away in the Spirit. God declared long ago that He would take the things of the Spirit and give them to *"babes and sucklings"*:

> *Out of the mouth of babes and sucklings hast thou ordained strength because of thine enemies, that thou mightest still the enemy and the avenger.*   Psalm 8:2

> *Howbeit when he, the Spirit of truth, is come, he will guide you into all truth: for he shall not speak of himself; but whatsoever he shall hear, that shall he speak: and he will show you things to come. He shall glorify me: for he shall receive of mine, and shall show it unto you. All things that the Father hath are mine: therefore said I, that he shall take of mine, and shall show it unto you.*   John 16:13-15

God delights in doing this, and you and I have no right to spurn or try to control people who are starving for the things of God. Stop spoon feeding them and let God have His way. If He wants to bring people quickly into many experiences, let Him do it. If He wants to feed His people by His Spirit, get out of the way and let Him do it. Let the river flow. Better yet, let it flow through you.

Too many of us miss the benefits of the river because we are afraid of it, afraid that things will get out of control, "out of order." We're afraid of things we can't control. But it doesn't matter if things get a little out of order. If God is in control, what are we worried about? Our order doesn't heal the sick and deliver the oppressed. It is time to let God institute His order among us. Rejoice in the liberty of the river.

The Lord Himself sets the pattern ... and that is why we must listen to the voice of the Spirit of God as He is speaking to us in our services.

The Lord Himself sets the pattern. You might say, "We can do it another way," but you're wrong! If God tells you to do it by laughing, you can't do it any other way. If He tells you to do it by giving, you can't do it another way. He sets the pattern, and that is why we must listen to the voice of the Spirit of God as He is speaking to us in our services. When He tells us what He will do if we do certain things, we must absorb every word. Then, just do what He said to do, and He will do what He has promised.

When Brother and Sister Roger Akers first came to work with us, they had come from a traditional Pentecostal background. They began to venture a little from the shoreline, until God began to open many wonderful doors to them. These are doors they could not possibly have entered if they had not allowed God to free them from the constraints of their background and to launch them out into the deep.

> **When the river is flowing, there is liberty, and if liberty is lacking, we know that the river is not present or that it is not being allowed to flow.**

When the river is flowing, there is liberty, and if liberty is lacking, we know that the river is not present or that it is not being allowed to flow.

All of the gifts of the Spirit are to be found in the

flow of the river. Some need to move into a prophetic flow, for it is part of the river.

It is up to us how much of the river's power we use. In the natural, we harness the power of rivers and use that power for many different purposes. It is the same in the Spirit. There is much power yet to be used.

We first allow the power of the river and the flow of the prophetic word to minister to us personally, and then we use it to bless others. First, we allow it to flow in and speak into our own spirit, and then we let it flow out of us and speak into the lives of others. There is something wonderful about being first partaker of that revelatory realm of the Spirit of God.

When you lay hands on someone for their healing, that healing flow touches every weak part of your own body and begins to heal any sickness within you.

Sometimes when you finish prophesying, those sounds are in your soul. Sometimes you feel the rhythms in your soul. Maybe for the rest of the night, even after you have gone to bed, you can hear the

Holy Ghost singing over and over. The words of the river echo and reverberate in your soul, washing over you, doing a work in your spirit. The flow touches you as well as those around you.

When you lay hands on someone for their healing, that healing flow touches every weak part of your own body and begins to heal any sickness within you. The river is coming from the very throne of God and flowing through you, and it quickens you and keeps you young. It becomes a fountain of youth within you. The fact that the person you are praying for is healed is just a bonus. You have partaken first.

No wonder we stay so young! So many people say to me, "Sister Ruth, I don't know how you keep up with your schedule." It isn't easy, getting on and off airplanes, in and out of airports, walking miles down those airport concourses. I couldn't do it in the natural. It is only as I stay in the anointing of the river that I can do it day after day.

That's just a beginning. Whatever you need, you can find it in *River Glory*.

Part III:

What Must I Do?

Chapter 19

Meet God in the River

There is a river, the streams whereof shall make glad the city of God, the holy place of the tabernacles of the most High. GOD IS IN THE MIDST OF HER; she shall not be moved: God shall help her, and that right early.

Psalm 46:4-5

"God is in the midst of her." Our God is extending to you an invitation to meet Him in the river. Accept His invitation and step into *River Glory* for your own life and for those around you. Accept His invitation and begin to declare gladness for the people of America, revival glory flowing from one side of this country to the other, from border to border, from sea to shining sea. The streams of God bring victory, for our nation, and for every other nation of the world.

God is in control of world events. He is the Triumphant One and desires to use us as those that speak triumph and speak victory. Accept His invitation today.

> No one need be afraid of this invitation. ... If the Lord says to you, "I'll meet you in the river," you are not going home now. He is just quickening you, anointing you, revitalizing you, enduing you with power from on high, putting a newness into your spirit, a newness into your walk, a newness into your talk, a newness into your life, so that you can rise up and do exploits.

God wants to meet us at the river. Some people might get a little nervous with an invitation like that. In the old days, the only thought people ever had about the river was crossing over to the other side, and that was not always the most pleasant thought. With an invitation like this, some would be afraid that they were going to die before morning.

One Easter Sunday morning in Jerusalem, we had a knock at the door rather early. It was an Orthodox priest who was certain that he was dying.

"Why do you think you're dying?" we asked.

"Oh," he said," I saw the Lord early this morning." In his thinking, seeing the Lord meant you were near death. We were happy to tell him that seeing the Lord these days means that you are about to enter into a new and wonderful life.

No one need be afraid of this invitation. Don't get nervous if the Lord says to you, "I'll meet you in the river." You are not going home now. He is just quickening you, anointing you, revitalizing you, enduing you with power from on high, putting a newness into your spirit, a newness into your walk, a newness into your talk, a newness into your life, so that you can rise up and do exploits. Meet God in the river.

There are miracles in the river, and God is saying to us, "I want you to get in the Spirit and stay in the Spirit." Get yourself completely immersed in this mighty river of God and stay under its life-giving influence. Don't be satisfied just to be touched by the Spirit, but allow the Spirit to overwhelm you. Let the river flood its banks, and overflow you continually.

On November 15, 1998, God had me draw an imaginary line on the platform where I was ministering and to jump over it. He had told us that He wanted us to be totally into the new by that date. I understand that others are being led to do the same thing.

Will jumping over an imaginary line really bring you into something new in God? Some probably think that is a very foolish thing to do, but believe me, it's not foolish if you see the line.

Jump from the old into the new. Jump from the bank of the river into the deep places. Jump from your own thinking into God's thinking. Jump from what you know into what you don't know. Jump from the realms of the past into the revelatory realms of the future.

God is doing new things in the river. He is performing miracles. He is bringing signs and wonders forth by the power of His Holy Spirit, and He is inviting you to participate.

When you can see the new thing God is offering you, it is not foolish to make the leap. The realm of His Glory is just as real as anything else you can see.

God is doing new things in the river. He is performing miracles. He is bringing signs and wonders forth by the power of His Holy Spirit, and He is inviting you to participate. You have a personal invitation from Him. His blessings are not just for one or two or a dozen. This invitation is for all. God wants you to meet Him in the river.

God is ready to meet us in the river, but it is up to us to accept the invitation. It is time to stop standing on the bank looking on. We must plunge in. For those less adventuresome ones who are afraid to plunge, walk on out into the depths of the waters of God. Start walking into it, taking one step after another, moving forward, allowing the Holy Spirit to measure it out for you.

When He has measured a thousand and you come into the place where your ankles are covered, don't stop there. Let Him measure a thousand more for you so that you can come into knee-deep waters. Don't stop there in the knee-deep water. Let the Spirit measure a thousand more for you and keep going out into deeper waters. The important thing is that you not stand forever at the water's edge. Come into the river, for the Lord has promised to meet you there.

Some people are afraid of water, but the Lord is removing our fears. Among the thousands of people I pray for in the course of a year, I am amazed at how many tell me they are afraid. "Don't be afraid," I tell them. "Just relax." Someone is always behind them to catch them when they fall, but I sense that it is not the physical part that causes them to be afraid. They are afraid of the plunge into the river of God. What a shame! We have nothing to fear in the river. He has promised to meet us there.

Yes, He will carry us out into realms we have never known, but trust Him. Let go of every fear. Don't be concerned about getting out too deep. Be concerned about not getting out deep enough.

Don't be concerned about getting out too deep. Be concerned about not getting out deep enough.

You can be peculiar and still not be in the river, so don't be afraid of peculiarity. Sometimes, the deeper people get in, the more normal they become. God puts some normalcy into those who have no normalcy in the natural. Their lives have been misshapen and filled with turmoil, but as they get into the river, God begins to put into action a healing process that will forever transform their lives. He brings normalcy to a life that has known none. While they are in the Spirit, way out in the depths of the river, God brings a healing to the body, a healing to the emotions and a healing to the mind. He gives them a new sense of direction and they know that they are going forward into the full purposes of God. What are you waiting for? Get into *River Glory* today.

Chapter 20

Step Into the Waters

And when the man that had the line in his hand went forth eastward, HE MEASURED A THOUSAND CUBITS, and he brought me through the waters; the waters were to the ankles.
Ezekiel 47:3

"He measured a thousand cubits." The river is here. Now step into the waters.

One of the great statements I have heard my Uncle Bill make concerning the river of God is that every time you step into the river you step into it in a new place because the river is constantly moving. You might step off of the bank at the exact same place as before, but the water is not the same because of the river's flow. Each time we step in, we find ourselves in new waters, and although we often find it difficult to step into something new or unfamiliar, God

will lead us forth into this revival by the revelation
of the Holy Spirit. Step boldly into the waters.

This river of God can be entered only by those who
humble themselves:

> *And whosoever shall exalt himself shall be*
> *abased; and he that shall humble himself shall*
> *be exalted.*   Matthew 23:12

You must descend to enter this river. It will carry
you to the heights, but your journey must begin by
going down, through humility. Sometimes the servants of God are the last to humble themselves. We
think that because we know so much about God and
because we have been used of Him in the past, we
know how to do things. It seems that we almost want
to tell God how to do His business sometimes. In
this revival, however, we are all on a level playing
field. God is doing it His way. Humble yourself and
let Him do it.

Beyond the need for humility, however, getting
into the realm of the heavenly, the realm of the glory
of God, is easier than most of us have imagined. It
comes through the simplicity of praising until the
spirit of worship comes and of worshiping until the
glory comes. When the glory comes, all we need to
do is yield ourselves and we will be carried away
by the flow of the river of God. It isn't hard. Just let
the river flow.

We get into the river by praising God, worshiping Him, dancing before Him, by yielding to the laughter of the Spirit, by laying aside our own thinking and focusing all our attention on the Lord. When we find that our mind is beginning to drift, we must focus on the Lord. We must learn to forget about ourselves and to concentrate on Him. When we do, before long, we are floating in the river, and nothing can compare with being in the river.

Nothing can compare with being in the river.

Somebody gave me a lovely pin last summer. It is one of those new ones that shows the river flowing and somebody dancing and praising the Lord on the top of the river. These pins and others like them are being marketed now because of what God is doing in the revival. Well, dancing on the river is a good start. When we really get into the river, we will not be seen by those around us.

"Where is Sister Ruth?" someone will ask.

"I don't see her," you will have to answer. "I can only see the river. She must be down there somewhere in the depths of it, but the water is so deep and the river is flowing so quickly that she is not visible to me."

I am content just to sit back and watch it happen and to say, "Praise the Lord! The river is here. Revival has come, the glory of God is being revealed, miracles are taking place, and God is doing it all by His Spirit."

It is much easier to experience the river in places where it is clearly flowing.

It is much easier to experience the river in places where it is clearly flowing. I encourage people everywhere I go to get to Brownsville/Pensacola and be part of the revival there. When revival breaks out, we need to visit places that are in revival and experience what God is doing.

In July of 1998 I was able to get to a morning meeting for pastors at the Assembly of God Church in Springfield, Virginia, where Brother Cover is pastor. Pastor John Kilpatrick was the speaker that morning. As he came into the sanctuary that morning there was a wave of glory that came in with him. I immediately began to cry because I was melted in his presence. I wondered why I was so melted, and the Lord told me that He wanted me to feel His heart's appreciation toward Brother Kilpatrick for the great sacrifices he has personally made for revival. It was a long way for him to come by bus, from Brownsville, Florida, to northern Virginia, for just two days of meetings, but Pastor Kilpatrick makes trips like that around the country nearly every week to help bring River Glory to the people of our land.

I frequently ask the people in the congregations I minister to if they have been to Brownsville, and I am amazed how many have not. When God is doing something, we must make the effort to get to the place where He is doing it. There are places we hear of where the river has broadened out a little more than in other places. It is not different water, but there is a broadness or perhaps a depth there that we are not experiencing in every place, and we want to experience that. Beat a path to places where revival is already in progress and, once there, get prayed for by those who are already in the water.

Something about the river is different there. Perhaps it is just that we have remained too close to the shoreline, been too cautious. When we go where others have made a transition from the bank into the depths of the waters and we see them launching out, it makes it easier for us to move out into those same depths of the flow of the river. That doesn't mean that the river is not flowing in our towns too, but too many of us have been enjoying paddling our feet in the water, when we should be out there swimming in the deeper places.

When we get among people who are all swimming, we say to ourselves, "What am I doing here,
just splashing my feet in the water, when I could be
swimming in the depth of the river too?" It makes
us willing to get out there and swim with them. God
has many amazing things to show us, but He is waiting for us to get out into those deeper waters.

When we get among people who
are all swimming, we say to ourselves, "What am I doing here, just
splashing my feet in the water,
when I could be swimming in the
depth of the river too?" It makes us
willing to get out there and swim
with them.

The revival in Brownsville began on Father's Day
in 1995, and the great revival in Smithton, Missouri,
began in March of 1996. Let revival begin today in
your heart and in your church. This is God's hour
and His river is flowing.

Some no longer have faith for revival in America.
They are sure that America is much too wicked to
be blessed by God, but I have faith that God will
not only restore the Christian foundations that have

been destroyed but will raise up an even greater spiritual edifice. When we step into the waters of God's river, He can do utterly amazing things in and through us.

It is not enough that the river is here. If you don't step into its waters, you will not benefit from its life-giving flow. The act of stepping into the water, therefore, is of utmost importance.

It is important that we be given opportunity to participate in the river and that we give others opportunity to participate. It is one thing to hear great sermons, but it is quite another thing to put into action what we are hearing. We each must be given a chance to flow in the river of God and to let the river flow through us. Revival is participation, and without participation, there can be no revival.

It is not enough that the river is here. If you don't step into its waters, you will not benefit from its life-giving flow. The act of stepping into the water, therefore, is of utmost importance.

It is impossible to know this river without experiencing it. You may know what it looks like. You may say:

"The colors are so beautiful."
"The water looks clear."
"It seems pure."
"It looks refreshing."
"It would be cooling on a hot day."

Imagining what it would be like is not the same as experiencing it. Describing the river is not enough. You cannot be a spectator in revival. Spectators may think they know what revival is about, but they don't.

A very strange attitude has arisen among many Christians. They are now very anti-experience oriented. They are very skeptical of every experience and want to examine it long and hard before seeking it themselves. How can this be? What God wants to do in us can only be known by experience. There is no other way.

When revival comes, everyone is suddenly awakened unto God in such a way that when He speaks in any dimension, we can respond immediately to His voice. If He urges us to dance, we can do it. If He encourages us to shout, we can respond. If His will is that we all clap together, we can clap. There is a corporate response to the Spirit of the Lord.

God is doing whatever it takes to free us quickly. What used to take many years, as we progressed through all the spiritual stages, is now being done in a very short time through the work of the Spirit. He is giving us a total immersion process. No part of us is excluded.

God is doing whatever it takes to free us quickly. What used to take many years, as we progressed through all the spiritual stages, is now being done in a very short time through the work of the Spirit. He is giving us a total immersion process. No part of us is excluded.

Some of us are still of the old order, and even when people have been immersed in the river and, as a result, have been set free, saved, filled with the Spirit and set on fire for God, we still want to begin at the beginning with them. It disturbs some Christians that new believers can come in without doing things in "the normal order."

When Peter was called to minister to the household of Cornelius and something new happened (the people were immediately filled with the Spirit and began to speak in tongues), he was not disturbed by that. He said:

Can any man forbid water, that these should
not be baptized, which have received the Holy
Ghost as well as we?   Acts 10:47

Peter did not insist that these people go back and
start with A, B, C. They had already come to know
the Lord and were filled with the Spirit. There was
no reason to take them backward. Some people are
still insisting that we learn 1, 2, 3, when God is already saying "98, 99, 100." This is a time of great
acceleration. Let God do it His way.

One brother who attended our summer campmeeting had been saved only a month, but his
deliverance was so great that he was already in
charge of a house ministry. God is doing a quick
work. In countries like Russia, where there has been
a severe shortage of qualified pastors, people who
are saved only a few months are already pastoring
successful churches. How can this be? Because there
is no one else to do it. Do they have all the answers?
Of course not, but they are in the river, and the river
is in them, and that's what is important.

My brother won a young man to the Lord in St.
Petersburg, Russia. When he went back there a year
or two later, that man was pastoring a church of
twelve hundred people. This phenomenon will only
increase in the days ahead. The river is flowing. Step
in.

Most rivers flow in only one direction, but don't expect the same of the river of life. One time it will flow in one direction, and the next time in another. The important thing is not to understand how the river flows but to get in and flow with it — whatever direction it is flowing at the moment. This is why it is so foolish for us to dictate to God how He does His miracles. This is a river of life. Step into its waters and let its life be ministered to you — in any way God sees fit.

Most rivers flow in only one direction, but don't expect the same of the river of life. One time it will flow in one direction, and the next time in another. The important thing is not to understand how the river flows but to get in and flow with it — whatever direction it is flowing at the moment.

Like Pastor Steve Gray in Smithton, Missouri, you don't have to *be* the revival. All you have to do is *host* the revival. The Lord is quite willing to be the river, if we are just willing to get in. What we don't understand He can teach us while we're in the river. Step in.

It may seem strange to some to call God's Spirit "the river." Well, call it what you want. Call it the river, the move, the revival or the awakening. It doesn't matter what you call it, but you can't be halfway into it. The river is not optional. We will not have several different classes of people in the move of God. You are either in or you are not in. Those who want to be in but not too much in will be left behind. Step into the water and get in the flow. The choice is yours. Step into the water. This is your opportunity.

Personally, I don't believe the baptism in the Holy Spirit is optional either. While I know that technically a person can get to Heaven without speaking in other tongues, without being baptized in the Spirit (because our fellowship is around the cross), I am sure that God will confront every denominational group before His coming and demand of them an answer as to whether or not they are willing to be baptized in His Spirit and speak in tongues. People who have taught against it and others who have not been open to it will be speaking in tongues more than the rest of us before it's over.

If we want to be in the move of God in the last day, we have a decision to make. Step into the water and experience *River Glory* for yourself.

Chapter 21

Launch Out Into the Deeper Places

Afterward he measured a thousand; and it was a river that I could not pass over: for the waters were risen, WATERS TO SWIM IN, a river that could not be passed over.

Ezekiel 47:5

"Waters to swim in ..." It is time we lose our fear of the river and get out into its life-giving flow, let its waters carry us away and begin swimming in God's Spirit in a new way.

In my book, *Revival Glory*, I mentioned the new and different strokes God has for each of us. Some have always done a particular stroke because they liked it, because it seemed easy for them or because they were comfortable with it. That's fine, but now God is showing us something new.

The thought of a new stroke seems threatening to

most of us because we don't do it quite as well yet as we do others. It is always easier to stick with the familiar and the comfortable. We always feel better doing something at which we can excel. That's understandable, yet God wants to bring us out into some new areas, areas we have never flowed in before. He is offering a new stroke for this new day, and if you are willing, He will teach you by His Spirit.

I put that in the book because one evening in our services I saw myself doing a side stroke. I never liked doing the side stroke, but since the day God showed me that I could do it, I have been doing some side strokes in the Spirit. I know that I sometimes look like a beginner, but that's okay. Swimming in this new way may not be altogether comfortable for me, but the Lord knows what He is doing. I am swimming on out into the greater *River Glory*.

We developed our own little style in the ankle-deep water, and when we felt challenged to move deeper, we didn't mind giving that up for another style in the knee-deep area. We changed again as we moved on into the loin-deep water. When we finally got around to serious swimming, for some reason our style got set in stone, and we are now slow to want to change it. When we know how much more there is to experience, however, it makes it far easier for us to be willing to change.

I was blessed to be in great revival services as a child, and I meet many people who have not had that same privilege. That experience gives me a certain advantage, but in this present revival we are all learning new things. There were things we experienced in the late forties and the fifties that have not yet been reached in this present revival, but God is also calling us out into new waters, into new experiences.

There is, within the souls of God's people these days, a greater and greater hunger for the things of His Spirit. This hunger will not allow us to rest in the shallow places. It is urging us to let go of the shore and be carried on out into greater things.

There is, within the souls of God's people these days, a greater and greater hunger for the things of His Spirit. This hunger will not allow us to rest in the shallow places. It is urging us to let go of the shore and be carried on out into greater things. What do we have to lose? Insisting on staying near the shoreline will only limit our experience in God. Launch out into the deep.

There is no way to prepare yourself for the depths of God's Spirit. You cannot ask someone else about their experience and then practice the strokes you may need to successfully swim there. You cannot, in any way, anticipate what you will experience in the depths of God's glory. There is only one way to experience it, and that is to get out there and start swimming.

We can no longer be content with our feet in the shallow waters. We can no longer be content to keep our feet on solid ground. It is time to move out of the realm of our understanding and see what God has for us. As long as we remain in the ankle-deep waters or the knee-deep waters or even the loin-deep waters, we are still able to touch bottom. We are still able to stand on our own two feet. We still feel self-reliant. Step out by faith. God wants to move you out into the unknown.

> Sometimes God has to allow something to knock us off our feet so that we can get out into the depths of the river and learn to flow with it.

Those who have a problem with stepping out by faith insist that they must stand on their own two feet. There is nothing wrong with that determination, but if you can always stand on your own two feet, you can never experience the depths of God's river. Sometimes God has to allow something to knock us off our feet so that we can get out into the depths of the river and learn to flow with it.

If you want to swim in the river, get ready to learn a new stroke or two. Let God broaden your experience. Each day, swim out a little farther than you did the day before. Test some new waters. Try something new in the Spirit. Let God lead you out into ever deeper waters.

When you get out deep enough, you will suddenly find yourself with the ability to believe for multitudes. Maturity in the realm of faith can only be reached in the depths of the river. We can talk about faith and preach about faith, but when we get into the depths of the river, we will suddenly know faith.

Swim on out. Don't be afraid to lose your contact with the shoreline. That doesn't mean, as some insinuate, that you will become worthless in this world. We are still here in this world for the moment, but although we are *in* it, we are certainly not *of* it. We have a higher calling. Move on out into the depths of the vastness of God's river.

God has some people He wants you to minister to, but you are not in the position right now to do it. You may know God and have some spiritual gifts in operation in your life. You may have certain ideas about which stroke is best to use in which circumstance, but you still have much to learn. God always does it differently than we anticipate. Launch on out into the deep water, and He will do the rest.

We can talk about faith and preach about faith, but when we get into the depths of the river, we will suddenly know faith.

God gets us out into waters that *"cannot be passed over,"* and suddenly we are seeing rabbis stepping into the waters of revelation. Suddenly whole synagogues are experiencing a move of God's Spirit. Suddenly we are being used to bless ministers who have never considered laying hands on the sick. Now, not only are they doing it, but great miracles are being performed.

When will all this happen? Just as soon as we can get over our fear of the water and let the Spirit carry us out into the deeper places.

Anyone who swims knows that you can't afford to go into deep water laden down by anything. Swimming with your clothes on is very difficult. Clothes get wet and heavy, and they will drag you down.

Some trained divers go into deep water with oxygen tanks and other diving gear, but that is something altogether different. If they just wanted to swim and be carried about by the waters, they would quickly rid themselves of anything that might weigh them down. We cannot afford to be burdened down by anything. God wants to set you free from every encumbrance. He wants to make you carefree. You can't swim right when you are loaded down with all sorts of additional baggage. Get rid of every weight, and swim on out into the greater glory.

The Hebrew word for glory is *kabowd*, and the root has the understanding of "weightiness." There is a "weight of glory" that we experience in our meetings. In order to experience this, however, we must be light, totally carefree, not weighed down by the cares of life. Toss every care to the Lord and be free to flow in the river of God. Let Him make you completely carefree.

The most important thing for us to concentrate on these days is making ourselves available for the present-day move of God, lightening the load, getting rid of every weight. Let us get ready to do some distance swimming in the river of God's glory.

If you have already stepped into the river, it is time to go a little deeper. Keep stepping in until you have found waters to swim in. Let God's Spirit carry you on out into deeper places.

Years ago, when Fuchsia Pickett had a church in Dallas, I had just finished preaching to her people one evening when the Lord spontaneously gave me a little song:

> *Why don't you let go and let God do what He wants to do in you?*

As the people began to "let go" the Spirit of God began to flow into our midst in a fuller way.

The Spirit gave me other verses to the chorus:

> *Why don't you let go and let God take you to the nations of the world?*
> *Why don't you let go and let God show you His glory?*

There is no limitation to what God can do for us if we can learn to let go and let Him have His way.

The message of the chorus is still valid. If you and I expect to receive the benefits of this vast river, we must let go and let the divine flow carry us away. We cannot hold back in fear. Yield yourself to the Lord with confidence.

The Spirit of God gave me another little chorus:

> *If you want to see the miracle flow, launch out.*
> *In the deep is the miracle flow. Launch out.*

How can we just stand on the shore
when others are already getting into
deeper waters? How can we afford
to refuse to jump in when others are
enjoying the benefits of the river? If
you want to see the miracle flow,
launch out into the deep.

How can we just stand on the shore when others are already getting into deeper waters? How can we afford to refuse to jump in when others are enjoying the benefits of the river? If you want to see the miracle flow, launch out into the deep.

There are treasures in the depths of the river. It is when we get into those depths that prophecy begins to flow and miracles begin to be manifested. The deeper we get in the water, the more profound these manifestations become until it is obvious that we are prophesying beyond our depth and seeing miracles beyond our grasp. We have moved beyond the realm of our own understanding, and no one can doubt that what is coming forth is by the Spirit of God. As we plumb the depths of the waters, we will find diamonds, rubies, sapphires and many other gems, the riches of the Kingdom of God with which we can bless the people. It only happens as that flow of revelation begins to come forth in the depths of the river. The river flows, and we must learn to flow with it. It flows because we are drinking deeply from the Source and we must never stop drinking of *River Glory* or the rivers will stop flowing from our innermost being.

Chapter 22

Sing and Dance Your Way Into the River

SING UNTO THE LORD A NEW SONG,
and his praise from the end of the earth, ye that
go down to the sea, and all that is therein; the
isles, and the inhabitants thereof.

Isaiah 42:10

"Sing unto the LORD a new song." One of the easiest ways of coming into the heavenly realm is singing in the Spirit and dancing in the Spirit.

When God began to teach us in Jerusalem about singing the new song, a young American couple with two boys had come to live with us. They wanted to go to South Africa, but they had encountered some problems with their finances. We raised money for the husband to go ahead, but the rest of the family had to stay behind and wait for him to send money from South Africa.

When God told us all to sing a song of faith, the others in our group were ready to travel in ministry. They knew exactly where they would be going, and their suitcases were packed. In the midst of the singing, however, this shy and quiet sister began to sing her song of faith. Her song was:

> *I once was a cocoon,*
> *But now I am a butterfly.*
> *I once was a cocoon,*
> *But now I am a butterfly.*
> *I'm flying!*
> *I'm flying!*
> *I'm flying!*

It may not have been the greatest hymn ever written, but suddenly the Spirit of God began to speak and the Lord said, "Because you stepped out in faith and said you are flying, go home and pack your bags. Before the week is out you *will* be flying." A great miracle took place that week so that the young mother and her two small boys could fly to South Africa and join her husband in ministry there. This is the day of the new song.

The Welsh revival was known for its songs. The miners marched into the mines singing, and it was said that their song could be heard far and wide. A new song came forth in the Azusa Street revival as well.

There is something about the new song that brings a release in ways that nothing else can. The move of the Spirit of God comes on the wings of song, and as some of you release your song to the Lord you will find yourself flowing in a new dimension of the Spirit, soaring in a new realm of the Spirit, moving in a new place in God.

There is something about the new song that brings a release in ways that nothing else can. The move of the Spirit of God comes on the wings of song, and as some of you release your song to the Lord you will find yourself flowing in a new dimension of the Spirit, soaring in a new realm of the Spirit, moving in a new place in God.

God is ready to bring forth the new song, but we must cooperate with Him. We need to yield to God, to believe for it and to step into it. Instead of always reaching out for the familiar, we can reach out into the unknown and let a prophetic flow come to us that gives us new words and new melodies with which to praise our God.

There is music and singing and a new song to be played and sung in the river, and it is for those who could not formerly carry a tune just as much as for the musically talented. Many of us are not musically inclined, but when God births a new song in the depths of our being, we can all break forth in singing.

The Apostle Paul wrote to the Corinthians:

> *I will sing with the spirit, and I will sing with the understanding also.*
>   1 Corinthians 14:15

God wants to release our songs in the Spirit and bring them forth in the realm of our understanding as well. He will do it for every one of us, if we will just let Him.

I can say that the new song has enriched my life in ways that nothing else, other than vision, has. The new song can open the treasure chests of Heaven and pour forth riches from our own mouths.

When we were learning to type in high school, we didn't always need to be seated at a typewriter to practice. We could be sitting almost anywhere, and our fingers would be moving on an imaginary keyboard, typing out the desired words. After we had learned the keyboard well enough, we no longer needed to do that. That same thing happened to me when we began learning to sing spontaneously. I sang about everything, and nearly drove some people crazy with my songs. Someone would say something to me, and when they did, a song was released within me, and I could not answer them in simple words. I had to sing my answer.

> I can say that the new song has enriched my life in ways that nothing else, other than vision, has. The new song can open the treasure chests of Heaven and pour forth riches from our own mouths.

In the days and weeks that followed, we prayed and worshiped together for many hours and never once did we reach back into the songs we already knew. We reached out into the unknown and began to sing songs we had never heard before. Some of those songs were very simple, yet they had a beauty and an anointing we had not experienced until then.

This is your day. God wants to place a new song within you and to cause your soul to break forth in singing.

Solomon was given one thousand and one songs.

The Song of Solomon or the Song of Songs, as it is known in Hebrew, was just the best known of those songs. There were many more.

God gave many songs to His people in Old Testament times. It is said in Hasidic circles that the Song of Songs, given supernaturally at the dedication of the Temple, was greater than the Temple itself. God is rejoicing over us with song, and He wants us to be able to reply and to sing spiritual songs unto Him.

During our camptime in the summer of 1998, we had a group of young people from an Assembly of God church in Toronto, Canada. One night one of the young men sang a song. He said, "Sister Ruth, after I read your book *Glory* God gave me this song." He stood up and began to sing it, and how blessed we were that instantly a young man had moved into the realm of spontaneous singing unto the Lord!

You might say, "Well I don't sing specials."

You should say "I didn't use to sing specials" because God is doing a new thing. He is birthing something wonderful within each of us. He is releasing a song within your soul. You may wake up with it one morning, or you may receive it as you are going to bed at night.

Sometimes new words may come to a song you already know. Sometimes my spirit wakes up singing some spiritual song I already know, but before long, God is giving me some new words for it.

I am continually aware of the need to step into a higher realm, to believe God for things we have not yet taken hold of, to step into things we have desired but have not yet experienced.

I had an interesting experience at the priests' conference. We had just finished singing a song, but the rhythm of the song was still in our bodies. Our mouths had ceased to work, but the heavenly rhythm was still with us, and we swayed with its movement. I was conscious in that moment that God was teaching us the rhythms of His river, the movement of its currents, the songs of His eternal realm, river songs.

A lovely Presbyterian pastor and his wife and family were with us at campmeeting in the summer of 1998. One night Brother Renny McClean was ministering on the new song. At the close of his message he had the people walking in a great circle, singing in the Spirit, waiting for the new song.

Suddenly the Presbyterian pastor began to sing a new song. His whole body was put into motion as he sang:

Neeeeeeeeeeew, sweeeeeeet, milk and honey, tabernacle music, flowing, flowing.

He repeated it, and it seemed that his hand was drawing the new out of his innermost being. His song brought forth great liberty and rejoicing in the service. I know that what God is doing is new, I know that it is sweet, I know that it is milk and honey, and I know that it is flowing. Since that time, I seldom use the word new without hearing it as that brother sang it that night.

While we are worshipping Him in the steps of the dance, the Lord is working changes within us and fine-tuning us to come into step with the realms of His glory. He is placing Heaven's tempo, Heaven's rhythm, Heaven's responses deep within our beings.

Can we trust the Lord for the new things that He wants to bring forth? Can we be yielded vessels in His hand and allow the glory to come forth upon our lips, with the new expressions that the Spirit of God wants to bring? Oh yes, I believe that God is going to raise up many anointed minstrels from among us. We will soon begin to hear of great songs that are being sung, and we will be forced to ask, "Where did the song writer get that song?" The answer will be that it came forth in the glory realm.

The prophet Zephaniah was moved to speak:

> *Sing, O daughter of Zion; shout, O Israel; be*
> *glad and rejoice with all the heart, O daughter*
> *of Jerusalem.*
> *The LORD thy God in the midst of thee is mighty;*
> *he will save, he will rejoice over thee with joy;*
> *he will rest in his love, he will joy over thee*
> *with singing.*   Zephaniah 3:14 and 17

Don't you love that? He is calling us to song, but He will also sing over those who are willing to sing to Him. If we are willing to rejoice, He will rejoice over us.

I have been declaring for several years now that this revival would be a singing revival, and I am on solid ground, for every great revival has been known by its song. I can go into a particular church and, by listening to the songs that are being sung, I can place that church in the history of revival. It doesn't take much insight to detect if their songs came from the revival of the fifties, for example, or of the sixties, the seventies, the eighties or the nineties. Each revival has brought forth a certain type of song. God is calling us all to sing a song that cannot be dated, a song that is fresh from His very throne. *"Sing a new song unto the Lord!"*

I notice that no matter how great a particular chorus might be, when we sing only the ones we already know, something is lacking in the service. When a new song comes forth by the Spirit, even if it seems to be a weak new song, there is a difference in the anointing and a difference in the glory present. I don't know how to explain it other than to say that the Lord delights in us when we are willing to step out into the new, when we are willing to get out of the boat and attempt to walk on the water.

When we reach out in the Spirit for new words and music with which to worship our Lord, suddenly there is a release of His Spirit that comes into our midst and wonderful things happen.

When we reach out in the Spirit for new words and music with which to worship our Lord, suddenly there is a release of His Spirit that comes into our midst and wonderful things happen. God wants to bring us all into areas of song beyond anything we have known in which suddenly, in the Spirit, we will hear the heavenly song and can mimic it, joining in and singing with the angelic hosts. In this way, we can bring to the Earth sounds that we are hearing in the heavenlies.

Jeremiah proclaimed:

Therefore they shall come and sing in the height of Zion, and shall flow together to the goodness of the LORD, for wheat, and for wine, and for oil, and for the young of the flock and of the herd: and their soul shall be as a watered garden; and they shall not sorrow any more at all.
                                        Jeremiah 31:12

The power is not in the voice; it is in the river.

What will they do *"in the heights of Zion"*? Sing. There is no easier way to get into the flow of the river. It doesn't matter if your voice is finely tuned or not. The power is not in the voice; it is in the river. There is a song that can be sung in the height of Zion that releases an anointing flow of the river of God upon those who hear it. *"Sing a new song unto the Lord!"*

When the river is flowing, God takes your voice, a voice that may have been used in the past to preach, to sing or to praise God, a voice you thought was already totally yielded to Him, and begins to do something altogether new. The Spirit possesses your throat and your mouth in a different way than you had ever experienced before. These experiences

need not be momentary. They can be eternal. From
that moment on, you can experience a new dimension.

The most "untuneful" person, when singing in the
glory, can sound like an opera star.

I was taken by Lady Astor to meet one of the
former members of Margaret Thatcher's cabinet at
his country home. We sat and visited a few minutes
as we shared wonderful cups of tea and delicious
English biscuits. When it seemed that it was time
for us to leave, he said, "Let me show you our country estate before you go."

We walked through the house until we came to a
room set aside as a chapel. There were two kneelers
and when he knelt at one, I knelt at the other. I softly
began praising the Lord and after a moment began
speaking in tongues. He was some four or five feet
away, and I encouraged him to do the same. In just
a moment he was speaking in other tongues, mag-
nifying the Lord. It was beautiful.

The tour of the house continued, and when we
got near the exit and were about to sign the guest
book, he turned to me and asked, "Will I be able to
do that again?"

I said, "Why don't you try it now."

He had never heard anyone sing in the Spirit before, but suddenly he began to sing as if he were a
trained opera singer. Utterly majestic sounds came

out of the depths of his being. He had no need of anyone teaching him what singing in the Spirit was about. The Holy Ghost knows the sounds of glory, knows the sounds of Heaven, knows the sounds of the river, the sound of many waters. How blessed I was in that moment!

Occasionally, when I have been passing through London, I have stopped to visit him in his townhouse near Harrods. I have noticed on the table a photo of him with the Queen mother, of him with the Queen, of him with the entire Royal Family, of him with other great personalities from around the world. Each time I visit, I say, "Let's do that again," and we start singing together in the Spirit.

Yes, these sounds of many waters will be heard in some of the finest estates around the world. They will be heard on Wall Street. They will be heard in the American Congress and Senate. We will hear the sounds of many waters echoing in places we never thought we would ever hear them.

If we can sing one simple chorus in the right way, the waters will come forth. When we are not entering into the flow of the river, there is somehow an over-sensitivity to noise that comes to us, and suddenly we notice someone whispering on the platform or something being moved that shouldn't be moved at that moment. When the river is flowing, we can all be noisy and no one notices any of these things.

When we are ministering to people, it is essential to let the river flow. I don't mind if the same chorus is sung over and over for two hours. We must not do anything that will hinder the flow of the river.

When we dance before the Lord, much more is being accomplished than most of us could ever imagine. While we are worshipping Him in the steps of the dance, the Lord is working changes within us and fine-tuning us to come into step with the realms of His glory.

When we dance before the Lord, much more is being accomplished than most of us could ever imagine. While we are worshiping Him in the steps of the dance, the Lord is working changes within us and fine-tuning us to come into step with the realms of His glory. He is placing Heaven's tempo, Heaven's rhythm, Heaven's responses deep within our beings. We must not be too busy to let this happen. We have no need to proceed in a particular way. When we are in God's presence, it is to have the pleasure of that presence, and it is that upon which we must concentrate, nothing else.

One morning I had a vision in which I saw the Lord as the processional God. I had never seen Him in exactly this way before and I began to declare what I saw. Suddenly all the people present got out of their seats and began to "process" around the hall where we were having the meeting. What a procession that was!

We Pentecostals have only known what we called the Jericho March. We always marched with the purpose of obtaining and declaring victory. Other groups have gone further in knowing the Lord as a ceremonial God, and they have "processed" as a means of rejoicing. We don't always need walls to fall down. There are times that we need to rejoice in the fact that the Lord is King. We can rejoice in His presence and rejoice in what He is doing.

> **There are times that we need to rejoice in the fact that the Lord is King. We can rejoice in His presence and rejoice in what He is doing.**

After a while some of those attending the conference joined in a circle and began to dance around. We were singing "There's a wheel within a wheel, and it's turning in me." I started to step up and have each person put his or her hand into the center of the wheel so that we could do a wheel dance, but as they touched my hand, one by one, the power of God was so strong that they instantly fell under it. There was no more dancing, for everyone was on the floor. What wonderful music and dancing and rejoicing we enjoyed together in that conference!

There is no quicker way to get into the depths of the river than by singing and dancing. Those who have tested the waters at our campground in Virginia can attest to this truth. Whatever you have to do, do it. Get into *River Glory* now. Don't wait.

Chapter 23

Laugh Your Way Into the River

THE VOICE OF JOY, AND THE VOICE OF GLADNESS, the voice of the bridegroom, and the voice of the bride, the voice of them that shall say, Praise the LORD of hosts: for the LORD is good; for his mercy endureth for ever: and of them that shall bring the sacrifice of praise into the house of the LORD. For I will cause to return the captivity of the land, as at the first, saith the LORD.   Jeremiah 33:11

"The voice of joy, and the voice of gladness ..." This is a revival of laughter, and if you can yield to the Spirit's desire in this regard, He will carry you into great release.

There has always been laughter in revival, but never quite in the measure we are experiencing it now. Today whole congregations are laughing. In former times we called it "holy laughter." A sister who attended our church when I was a child was known for her holy laughter. Later, there were others. Now, however, everyone is laughing.

> **When laughter wells up within us, I am convinced that God is enlarging our river beds and making room for a greater flow of His Spirit.**

The seat of laughter is the belly, and that also is the seat of the Holy Spirit in us. When laughter wells up within us, I am convinced that God is enlarging our river beds and making room for a greater flow of His Spirit. He is giving us greater abilities to yield to the Spirit, making more room for the river to flow. Just a trickle or a small stream is not enough. We need *rivers of living water*, *streams in the desert*.

One night in Summer Campmeeting one of the sisters said to me, "I have laughed until I have pains in my stomach from muscles I haven't used in years." She was being enlarged in her ability to yield to the Spirit of the living God. She was allowing God to do a new thing in her. She was allowing Him to release something deep within her spirit. She wasn't worried about how to do it. She was just letting it flow.

When we have yielded to the Spirit of laughter, often the enemy tries to tell us that we have done it ourselves. Why is that? Hardly anyone speaks in tongues without having to listen to this accusation. We are not smart enough to speak in tongues without the enablement of the Holy Ghost, and we cannot laugh uncontrollably without the Spirit's inspiration.

I lived in foreign countries for forty years of my life, and if I could have mimicked languages that easily, I would have been the best linguist in the world. Languages are not all that easy to pick up. You can hear a person speak something in another language and try to repeat it immediately and fail. How, then, can the devil say that we are just doing it on our own?

Laughter comes to us in the same way speaking in tongues does. You have to yield to it, or it won't happen. Some people believe that laughing is sovereign, that we cannot control it, cannot help ourselves. It is often a sovereign experience the first time it comes to us, but after that we must yield ourselves to it.

Some people are sovereignly filled with the Holy Ghost without ever having sought the experience. I was not one of them. I was actively seeking this blessing. I learned that one of my best friends had received the Holy Ghost the Saturday before and that another of my best friends had received the Holy Spirit on Thursday night, and by that next Saturday I was determined that no matter what I was going to receive the Holy Spirit. I was only nine years old at the time, but God saw the hunger of my heart and filled me. It can come sovereignly or it can come through a concerted effort on our part. Don't let the enemy intimidate you and make you think that what you have is not from God.

When speaking of the restoration of Jerusalem, the Scriptures tell over and over of *"the voice of joy and ... gladness, the voice of the bridegroom, and the voice of the bride."* Laughter is part of this great voice of rejoicing.

There are things that we must give voice to. They are there; we just need to let them out.

There are things that we must give voice to. They are there; we just need to let them out. Some might object to the comparison, but it's a little like priming a pump. You keep a little water back to pour into it, and then when you start pumping, it doesn't take long for the water to start flowing.

"Can you give a scripture for that?" someone might ask. Yes. David had the secret:

And David was greatly distressed; for the people spake of stoning him, ... but David encouraged himself in the LORD his God.

1 Samuel 30:6

Laugh your way right into the depths of the river.

There are many ways to lend encouragement to what God is doing in your life. Sometimes, when the Lord tells you to rejoice and you don't feel like rejoicing, you have to prime the pump a little. When you do, suddenly the river begins to flow out of *"the innermost part of your being,"* and sometimes it manifests itself in holy laughter. Give vent to it and laugh your way right into the depths of the river.

God is doing things differently than we could have anticipated. If I had known that He was about to give me holy laughter, I think I would have made a point of attending some conferences where it was happening to hear all the different types of laughter and to choose the kind I wanted. I would certainly not have chosen the kind of laughing voice I got, but that's God's business. I intend to keep right on laughing my way into the depths of *River Glory*.

Chapter 24

Get Rivers of Living Water in You

In the last day, that great day of the feast, Jesus stood and cried, saying, If any man thirst, let him come unto me, and drink. He that believeth on me, as the scripture hath said, OUT OF HIS BELLY SHALL FLOW RIVERS OF LIVING WATER. (But this spake he of the Spirit, which they that believe on him should receive: for the Holy Ghost was not yet given; because that Jesus was not yet glorified.) John 7:37-39

"Out of his belly shall flow rivers of living water." God has promised that out of the *"belly,"* from deep within, from the depths of our innermost being, *"rivers of living water"* would flow, and if we are thirsty for revival it will happen. It is the thirst, Jesus showed us, that inspires His response.

We urgently need for the Lord to put the "saltiness" back in His people so that a thirst for righteousness will be created in those around us. He has called us to be the *"salt of the earth."* When the salt has lost its strength, people can be around us and still not feel thirsty for God. He wants to put the strength back into the salt so that when we tell the miracles of God and declare His presence and speak of revival, the telling of it will have the desired affect. Let a hunger be created within God's people everywhere, for it is that thirst that moves the heart of God.

Desire makes people travel long distances to receive God's touch upon their lives. It causes them to push aside the nonessentials so that they can have God's best.

Far too many churches are spiritually comfortable. They have no desire to go deeper. The people are satisfied. Their programs seem to be working, with everything seemingly in order. Revival, at that moment, would almost seem to be an imposition, a disturbance. Oh, let the saltiness come.

We may feel fully satisfied one minute, but when the saltiness of the Spirit is manifested, suddenly we want more. We want what God has done for others to happen to us. We want what is happening in other churches to happen in ours. We want what other cities have experienced to come to our city as well. When we declare the goodness of God and speak of revival, we are creating this desire in the hearts of others, and it is to this desire that God responds.

Desire makes people travel long distances to receive God's touch upon their lives. It causes them to push aside the nonessentials so that they can have God's best. If you are not thirsty for more of God, get into a good meeting where people are talking about the miracles of God and where the presence of God can be felt.

Fasting is another wonderful way to stir up your thirst. By fasting, you will not only develop physical thirst, but you will also develop a spiritual thirst for the greater things of God. "If you are genuinely thirsty," Jesus was saying, "I will give you something to quench that thirst."

What Jesus said seems too simplistic to many. Could it really be all that easy? Absolutely! The thirst is the hard part. Once you are thirsty, the rest is easy. Just come to Him and drink. It could not be simpler.

Some people have known this portion of scripture all their lives, but they are still not doing the simple things it requires. We may feel thirsty, but sometimes we are not coming to the Lord, and often we are not drinking or we are not drinking enough.

"Well, how long do you have to drink?" someone might ask. Until rivers of life start flowing out of your innermost being. You can't stop until it happens. Drink, drink and keep on drinking until those rivers are flowing. If there is no more than a trickle flowing out of you, you are not drinking enough. Even when a river is coming forth from you, don't stop drinking. God has ordained that *"rivers"* flow from you to bless the nations. Drink until it happens.

> **It is not enough that the river comes down from Heaven. It is not enough that it is in the church or in the conference or in the revival center. God wants it to flow through you. Until it is coming forth from your innermost being, He is not satisfied.**

It is not enough that the river comes down from Heaven. It is not enough that it is in the church or in the conference or in the revival center. God wants it to flow through you. Until it is coming forth from your innermost being, He is not satisfied.

It is not enough that others experience revival. It is not enough that your city be stirred. God wants revival fires to burn within you.

Rivers require channels or riverbeds through which they can flow, and we must be those channels. If we expect God's river to flow into the desert places of this world, we must provide the channel for it to flow through. If we want the river to go into the dry and parched places, you be the bed through which it can flow there. Multitudes await the delivering power and the healing virtues of the river of God. Will you be the channel God uses to bring it to them? Stop worrying about how unholy this world is and start making yourself a channel of God's holiness. Oh, let the thirst that will produce it come to us now.

Christians of all denominational backgrounds are thirsty for more of God, and sometimes that thirst is misunderstood. I have had fine ministers call me and ask what was wrong with them. Why were they feeling so dissatisfied? Why were they so miserable when God has been so good to them? They were interpreting the feeling they had inside as frustration, when it was not frustration at all. It was a thirst for more of God. Thirst is not a bad thing. It leads us to the river where we can drink our fill.

Don't ever let this thirst be quenched. Some who once knew the river no longer know it. They are not in the river, and the river is not in them. They can still preach a good sermon, but somehow the flow of healing for the nations is no longer present. What happened to these people? They got too satisfied with life. They became too content. Thirst creates in you a restlessness, an unease, that drives you to keep drinking more and more. When you stop drinking, the river stops flowing.

When you stop drinking, the river stops flowing.

When we hear men and women who have inspired and challenged us in the past, too often we are now disappointed. What they are saying may seem to be correct and good, but it no longer thrills our souls. It is apparent that they are no longer in the river. Many great Gospel singers who have blessed us in the past no longer stir us. At some point they stopped drinking from the river, and the difference in their song is noticeable.

God told us that He was tired of old voices trying to say new things. He wants new voices to say new things, therefore our voices must be transformed by the fresh touch of the river.

Once we have experienced the river, we can no

longer be satisfied with anything else. No artificial waters can quench our thirst. No substitute will meet our need.

"But how do we drink?" someone might ask. Well, how do you drink in the natural? You put the cup to your lips, you let the water flow into your mouth and you swallow. You don't even have to think about it. It's automatic, natural. You just take the water in.

Once we have experienced the river, we can no longer be satisfied with anything else. No artificial waters can quench our thirst. No substitute will meet our need.

How do we do that same thing in the presence of the Lord? First, we have to be there; then we open our mouths; and then we have to start taking it in and we have to keep taking it in until we are satisfied and until the rivers of living water are flowing from us. Don't make it complicated. It is as easy as breathing.

How do we get the river of God flowing? By drinking and drinking some more. If we will do the drinking, He has promised to do the rest. You be faithful to drink in the life-giving water, and God will be faithful to put a river in your *"belly."*

Once we become adept at drinking, our next challenge is to let the river flow out of us. Jesus said, *"Out of his belly shall flow rivers of living water."* The flow is essential. We have tried to contain it and have become a Dead Sea as a result. The Dead Sea is lovely, but it won't support life. Having an inlet without having an outlet is a recipe for disaster. Let the rivers flow. Stopped up or dammed up rivers are dangerous.

I don't mind it when people are a little jerky as they try to learn to let their rivers flow. At least they are trying. At least there is some flow. At least they are not turning into Dead Seas. In time, they will learn to remove all the obstacles to the river's flow. In time they will allow the Lord to remove the dams that men have built up to keep the river in check.

Many things that we do dam up the river. Our sense of respectability is often the greatest culprit, and God has to blast it away to get the waters moving again. So many of us are terrified of the idea of things getting out of hand in our services. Jesus said, *"Where the Spirit of the Lord is, there is liberty"* (2 Corinthians 3:17). How could the liberty produced by the presence of the Spirit of God ever be offensive? If we refuse to give the Holy Spirit the right to work in our midst, how can anything of eternal worth be accomplished? Learn to do what He wants to do when He wants to do it and how He wants to do it, and your rivers will always be flowing.

A brother who comes to our services occasionally is moved to do cartwheels. I like that. I have found no biblical prohibition to doing cartwheels in church. The lame man who was healed at the Beautiful Gate responded by: *"walking, and leaping, and praising God"* and he did it *"in the temple"* (Acts 3:8).

We can't be sure if there was a Hebrew word for cartwheels or not. This man may have done a few. Let the river flow. Don't allow your own thinking to dam it up. Don't quench the Holy Spirit of God. Let the waters flow from your innermost being.

A very learned man recently paid me a great compliment. He said: "You have the greatest gift of simplicity." I rejoiced in that.

Revival is here. Drink deeply. It is not enough to drink once. We must drink and drink and drink and drink some more.

God is calling for simplicity. There is no way to complicate His words: *"If any man thirst, let him come unto Me and drink. ... out of his belly shall flow rivers of living water."* That's about as simple as you can get, yet that teaching will last you until Jesus comes, for there is no limit to this river. It has no end. If we allow it to keep flowing, it will nourish us more and more. You cannot know its bounty until you get into its waters.

Revival is here. Drink deeply. It is not enough to drink once. We must drink and drink and drink and drink some more. Drink of God's presence. Drink of His glory. Drink of His greatness. No one else can do it for you. You must do it for yourself. We can bring you to the edge of the water and make it known to you, but you must make a conscious effort to drink.

When Gideon was faced with the need to choose men for his army, God told him to choose them by how they drank. I believe that this will also be the method of choosing God's soldiers in these last days. In the days ahead we will drink our way into the miraculous, into the supernatural realms.

A lady was attending our campmeeting who was a recovered alcoholic. She laughed when we sang a little chorus about taking another drink. "For the first time," she later told me, "I could sing those words and know that it was all right. I am no longer addicted to alcohol. I am addicted to the Holy Spirit, and I can take another drink."

There is revival in the river of God. Drink deeply of *River Glory*.

Chapter 25

Let the River Flow

Afterward he measured a thousand; and it was a river that I could not pass over: for THE WA-TERS WERE RISEN, waters to swim in, a river that could not be passed over.

Ezekiel 47:5

"The waters were risen." The river is here, and it is flowing. What must each of us do to receive its blessings? Let it flow.

When the river is present, you don't necessarily need to preach about it. Just let it flow. It is not always necessary to point it out and tell people to get in. Just let if flow. You get in, and others will follow you in.

This is God's river. You can't control it, and you can't dictate where and how it will flow. It will flow as God wishes it to flow. Stop resisting the currents of the river and let yourself be carried away with it. Let the river flow.

Just when we think we "have a handle on things," God changes the way He does things, and He does it to let us know that He is God and that what He does is done by His Spirit and not by the understanding of man. This is God's day, and He has every right to do things in His own way. This is God's revival, and only He has a right to say how it happens. This is His river. Stop resisting it and get with the flow.

The river itself suddenly takes over, and we find ourselves being carried away by the greatness of it.

God is changing us. He is changing our perceptions, and He is changing our abilities. He is causing us to take off the former garments and cast them aside and to put on the new garments of His righteousness and of His glory. He is causing us to embrace this last-day outpouring of the Spirit, the flow of His river.

Forget about trying to control everything. When we are only in ankle-deep or knee-deep or loin-deep, we are still in control, but when we begin to swim on out into the deeper waters of this great river, the river itself suddenly takes over, and we find ourselves being carried away by the greatness of it. We find ourselves doing things we never planned to do and things we never imagined ourselves doing. It's happening. Pastors, you can kick and resist revival all you want, but it's coming anyway. This river cannot be stopped. Let it flow.

> While you are struggling so hard to stay connected, God is doing everything He can to get you "unconnected."

Some have gone beyond the shoreline and have actually begun to swim around a bit in these waters, but most of us have not yet done any long-distance swimming in God's river. Most have not yet moved out into the deeper waters He provides. We're still splashing around in the shallows, but it is time to go deeper. In this hour, the Lord is moving us out into deeper waters by His Spirit. He is moving us into realms we have never experienced. Stop fighting the currents of the Spirit, and let it happen.

Some are clinging desperately to the shore, not willing to be carried away. This is what the Scriptures describe as *"halt[ing] between two opinions."* You cannot have the depths of the Spirit and physical security at the same time. You cannot go with the flow of God and remain connected to the Earth, to the familiar, to the traditional. You cannot have greater things in God and stay with what you already know, what you are already moving in. While you are struggling so hard to stay connected, God is doing everything He can to get you "unconnected." Let go. Let Him have His way. Let the river flow.

When the river is present, you don't necessarily need to preach about it. Just let it flow. It is not always necessary to point it out and tell people to get in. Just let it flow. You get in, and others will follow you.

The most wonderful thing about this river is that it can carry you. Your particular style is not the important thing. Your particular method is not the focus. Focus on the river, and let it bring you into new things. You have barely tasted the deep things of God. He has much more in store for you. Let yourself go and be carried on out in the deeper things of the Spirit.

Personally, I want to swim out into the deepest parts of the river. I want to have more of the same experiences John had on the Isle of Patmos. I want to have more of the same experiences Isaiah had in his day. I want to have more Pauline experiences and be lifted up into places where I cannot decide if I am in the body or out of the body. I want to be fully equipped for this last-day harvest, and that can only happen as I allow the river to flow and to carry me out into deeper waters.

Right now, wherever you happen to be, just give yourself to the Spirit, yield yourself to the the river just a little bit more, and allow yourself to be carried away.

We can always think of many people who need a message like this, but the truth is that you need it and I need it. Just about the time I think I am willing to do a new stroke, the Lord tests me, and I find I would still rather do it just like I have been doing it over time. He is accepting no excuses. He demands that we come out of the area of the familiar, out of our comfort zones, and that we be willing to step boldly into the flow of *River Glory.*

THERE IS A RIVER, the streams whereof shall make glad the city of God, the holy place of the tabernacles of the most High. God is in the midst of her; she shall not be moved: God shall help her, and that right early.

Psalm 46:4-5

And when the man that had the line in his hand went forth eastward, he measured a thousand cubits, and he brought me through the waters; the waters were to the ankles. Again he measured a thousand, and brought me through the waters; the waters were to the knees. Again he measured a thousand, and brought me through; the waters were to the loins. Afterward he measured a thousand; and IT WAS A RIVER that I could not pass over: for the waters were risen, waters to swim in, A RIVER that could not be passed over.

Ezekiel 47:3-5

In the last day, that great day of the feast, Jesus stood and cried, saying, If any man thirst, let him come unto me, and drink. He that believeth on me, as the scripture hath said, out of his belly shall flow RIVERS OF LIVING WA-TER. (But this spake he of the Spirit, which they that believe on him should receive: for the Holy Ghost was not yet given; because that Jesus was not yet glorified.)

John 7:37-39

And he showed me A PURE RIVER of water of life, clear as crystal, proceeding out of the throne of God and of the Lamb.

Revelation 22:1

Books by Ruth Ward Heflin

River Glory   ISBN 1-884369-87-1 . $13.00

Glory	English Edition	ISBN 1-884369-00-6 ... 10.00
	Spanish Edition	ISBN 1-884369-15-4 ... 10.00
	French Edition	ISBN 1-884369-41-3 ... 10.00
	German Edition	ISBN 1-884369-16-2 ... 10.00
	Swedish Edition	ISBN 1-884369-38-3 ... 10.00
	Finnish Edition	ISBN 1-884369-75-8 ... 10.00

Revival Glory   ISBN 1-884369-80-4 ... 13.00

Jerusalem, Zion, Israel and the Nations
                ISBN 1-884369-65-0 ... 13.00

Ask for them at your favorite bookstore or from:

Calvary Books
11352 Heflin Lane
Ashland, VA 23005
(804) 798-7756

www.revivalglory.org

God of Miracles

Eighty Years of the Miraculous

by Edith Ward Heflin

"My life has been very exciting because I was always looking forward to the next miracle, the next answer to prayer, the next thing Jesus would do for me. I expect I have lived twenty lifetimes within these eighty years. The God of all miracles has been so good and so very gracious to me."

– Edith Heflin

As you become witness to a life that has spanned the period from Azusa Street to this next great revival, the life of a unique woman who has known the great ministries of our century and has herself lived the life of the miraculous, you too will encounter the God of Miracles.

ISBN 1-56043-043-5 .... $10.00

Ask for them at your favorite bookstore or from:

Calvary Books
11352 Heflin Lane
Ashland, VA 23005
(804) 798-7756
www.revivalglory.org

Hear the Voice of God

by
Wallace H. Heflin, Jr.

* Does God still speak to His people as He did to the prophets of old?
* If so, how does He speak?
* Can we actually hear His voice?
* What can we do to become more sensitive to God's voice?

Wallace Heflin Jr. spent a lifetime hearing the voice of God and following God's directives in dynamic ministry to the people of this nation and the world. In this manuscript, the last one that he prepared before his death in December of 1996, he challenges us that not only is it possible to hear the voice of God, but that God actually extends to every one of us an invitation to commune with Him.

ISBN 1-884369-36-7 .... $13.00

Ask for them at your favorite bookstore or from:

Calvary Books
11352 Heflin Lane
Ashland, VA 23005
(804) 798-7756
www.revivalglory.org

The Power of Prophecy

by
Wallace H. Heflin, Jr.

"Of all the nine gifts of the Spirit, prophecy is the gift that God is using most to bring in the revival of the end-time. Because of that, it is prophecy that is being opposed now more than any other gift. I want to declare that it is time to take the limits off the gift of prophecy and off the prophets God has raised up for this hour. It is time to move into God's plan of action to declare His will prophetically to this, the final generation."

– Rev. Wallace Heflin, Jr.

- What is prophecy?
- What does it accomplish?
- Who can prophesy?
- How can YOU get started prophesying?

These and many other important questions are answered in this unique and timely volume.

ISBN 1-884369-22-7 .... $10.00

Ask for them at your favorite bookstore or from:

Calvary Books
11352 Heflin Lane
Ashland, VA 23005
(804) 798-7756
www.revivalglory.org

Other books
by
Rev. Wallace H. Heflin, Jr.

A Pocket Full of Miracles	0-914903-23-3	7.00
Bride, The	1-884369-10-3	7.00
Jacob and Esau	1-884369-01-4	7.00
The Potter's House	1-884369-61-8	9.00
Power In Your Hand	1-884369-04-9	8.00
Power In Your Hand (*Spanish Edition*)	1-884369-04-9	6.00

Ask for them at your favorite bookstore or from:

Calvary Books
11352 Heflin Lane
Ashland, VA 23005
(804) 798-7756
www.revivalglory.org

The BESTSELLING:

GLORY

by
Ruth Ward Heflin

What is Glory?

- *It is the realm of eternity.*
- *It is the revelation of the presence of God.*
- *He is the glory! As air is the atmosphere of the Earth, so glory is the atmosphere of Heaven.*

Praise ... until the spirit of worship comes. Worship ... until the glory comes. Then ... stand in the glory. If you can capture the basic principles of praise, worship and glory which are outlined in this book – so simple that we often miss them – you can have anything else you want in God.

ISBN 1-884369-00-6 .... $10.00

Ask for them at your favorite bookstore or from:

Calvary Books
11352 Heflin Lane
Ashland, VA 23005
(804) 798-7756
www.revivalglory.org

The BESTSELLING:
REVIVAL GLORY

by
Ruth Ward Heflin

What is Revival Glory?

- *It is standing in the cloud and ministering directly from the cloud unto the people.*
- *It is seeing in to the eternal realm and declaring what you are seeing.*
- *It is gathering in the harvest, using only the tools of the Spirit.*
- *It is, ultimately, the revelation of Jesus Christ.*

One cannot have revival without the glory or the glory without having revival.

ISBN 1-884369-80-4 .... $13.00

Ask for them at your favorite bookstore or from:

Calvary Books
11352 Heflin Lane
Ashland, VA 23005
(804) 798-7756
www.revivalglory.org

Jerusalem, Zion, Israel and the Nations

by
Ruth Ward Heflin

"God is returning the focus once again to Jerusalem. The place of beginnings is also the place of endings. And God's endings are always glorious.

"This overview is by no means definitive but an unfolding of scriptures coming into prominence in these days. As Moses saw the Promised Land from Nebo, one sees the world from Jerusalem."

– Ruth Heflin

ISBN 1-884369-65-0 .... $13.00

Ask for them at your favorite bookstore or from:

Calvary Books
11352 Heflin Lane
Ashland, VA 23005
(804) 798-7756
www.revivalglory.org

Calvary Pentecostal Tabernacle

11352 Heflin Lane
Ashland, VA 23005

Tel. (804) 798-7756
Fax. (804) 752-2163
www.revivalglory.org

8 ½ Weeks of Summer Campmeeting 1999

Friday, July 2 – Sunday night, August 29
With two great services daily, 11 A.M. & 8 P.M.

Ruth Heflin will be speaking nightly the first ten days and each Friday and Saturday night during Summer Campmeeting

Winter Campmeeting 2000

February 4 – 27

Ruth Heflin will be speaking nightly the first week and each Friday and Saturday night during Winter Campmeeting

Revival Meetings

Each Friday night, Saturday morning, Saturday night and Sunday night with Sister Ruth Heflin in all other months

Ministry tapes and song tapes are also available upon request.

Mount Zion Miracle Prayer Chapel

13 Ragheb Nashashibi
P.O. Box 20897
Sheikh Jarrah
Jerusalem, Israel

Tel. 972-2-5828964
Fax. 972-2-5824725
www.revivalglory.org

Prayer Meetings:

2:00 – 3:00 P.M. Daily
Monday – Thursday

Services:
Friday, Saturday and Sunday
10:30 A.M.
7:30 P.M.
Pre-meeting praise 7:00 P.M.

Come and worship with us in Jerusalem!